The Me'chus Dynasty

The Fantasy of a Heart Becomes a True Story

☙❧

Copyright©2014 - Anita DeMeulenaere -All rights reserved.

ISBN# 978-0-615-15034-5

Contact Information:

Email: mad63@comcast.net

Storefront: www.lulu.com./spotlight/mad63

Preface

As the car turned the corner, all I could see was an endless landscape that seemed to go on forever. There was fencing to mark the territory, but the view was breath taking. The hills rolled, the water ran, and the massive trees were what my eyes were seeing, going on until they were out of sight.

My thoughts rambled as I was still trying to absorb the way my life has changed in what I see as a short time. The inheritance received from my Aunt Millie and Uncle Nick was more than I could ever have imagined. The times spent with them has entwined memories that are unforgettable. Having their life come to a conclusion with death at this time from a truck accident was so unexpected. I did not think we would be burying them so young. He was only sixty-five, she was 63 and I have been a part of their life for most of my life.

Being that I am an only child, my father was close to his brother, Nick. I would spend the summers with them on school break. My Aunt Millie was wonderful also, so I had a second family of my own. I cannot imagine life without either of them.

Inheriting the Me'chus Ranch, a family name, includes the property, home, stable, and all that went with maintaining their home. I have grown up in their life so everything is a part of me. My feelings cross between overwhelmed at the responsibility and the loss of their lives. This all happened suddenly and here I am to claim what has been given to me.

I will introduce you to those who have so much meaning to me in my life on the ranch and tell you the stories surrounding their existence as they relate to me. Uncle Nick and Aunt Millie started with the purchase of some land and it developed into a Dynasty. Everything acquired has been a blessing of God and wonderful help from those close to them. The wonderful Barter System was in place meaning that each one would help and or exchange what they had; in return they would give what they had to offer to others.

God tells us in Scripture that we are to love Him first and then our neighbor. What better way to do this by helping your neighbor succeed and your reward to Him is your success. Love is an action word and so that will result in truth. If you are true to your neighbor, you will be true to yourself.

-Anita DeMeulenaere

Table of Contents

CHAPTER 1: The Me'chus Dynasty — Pg. 9
- a. A life long Dream — Pg. 9
- b. My Aunt and Uncles Ranch — Pg. 11
- c. The Inheritance — Pg. 16

CHAPTER 2: My Family — Pg. 19
- a. Possession of my Inheritance — Pg. 19
- b. Lucky Jo — Pg. 22
- c. Kelly — Pg. 25
- d. Fudzer — Pg. 29
- e. Robert — Pg. 32

CHAPTER 3: The River — Pg. 33
- a. Enjoying its Beauty — Pg. 33
- b. Swimming / Diving — Pg. 34
- c. Fishing — Pg. 35
- d. Canoeing — Pg. 38

CHAPTER 4: The Inhabitants of the property — Pg. 41
- a. The Indian Family — Pg. 41
- b. The Animals of the Environment — Pg. 44
- c. The Wild Horses — Pg. 53

CHAPTER 5: The Trip — Pg. 63
- a. Off to the Fair — Pg. 63
- b. The Accident — Pg. 65
- c. Help Arrives — Pg. 67
- d. The Damage — Pg. 70

    e. Going Home .... Pg. 75
CHAPTER 6: The Boys and Girls Club .... Pg. 81
    a. Learn to Work Together .... Pg. 81
    b. Taking Care of the Horses .... Pg. 85
    c. Riding Lessons .... Pg. 88
    d. Special Needs Children .... Pg. 94
CHAPTER 7: Horses to Ride / Horses to Roam ... Pg.101
    a. Horses Came with the Ranch Pg.101
    b. Horses as Auction Pg.113
    c. Horses Running Wild and Majestic Pg.120
CHAPTER8: Rehabilitating Horses Pg.123
    a. Race Horses Pg.123
    b. Injured Horses Pg.124
    c. Emotionally Disturbed Horses Pg.125
CHAPTER 9: Camping in the Mountains Pg.129
    a. The Requirements Pg.129
    b. Basic Training / Climbing Pg.130
    c. Assigned a Horse Pg.131
    d. Prepare Food and Supplies Pg.133
    e. The Camping Trip Pg.135
CHAPTER 10: Some More Fun Pg.151
    a. The Parade Pg.151
    b. The Apple Orchard Pg.152
    c. The Pumpkin Patch Pg.153
    d. The Christmas Tree Cutting Pg.154
    e. The Wagon Rides Pg.155

CHAPTER 11: My Aunt and Uncle Would be Proud
- a. Lucky Jo   Pg.158
- b. Kelly and Fudzer   Pg.158
- c. Robert   Pg.159
- d. Me   Pg.159
- e. The Perfect Place   Pg.161

CHAPTER 1: The Me'chus Ranch

A Life Long Dream

When growing up, we all think about life and what is ahead of us. Some are Possibilities and some are realities. We set goals to make a path to stay in the infinity mode. This does not mean failure but it may mean disappointment. Our thoughts can be attainable and some stay out of our reach. We all have to believe because our nature is to grow and achieve; become something to hopefully contribute to life. Our existence needs to matter and have an impact on someone or many to feel successful as a human being.

As a child, I would contemplate about many things but one desire was to have a ranch, with horses, land as far a the eye could see, and enjoy life to its fullest. I have an inborn passion for horses so life to me would have to involve horses to complete that vision. It would be in a ranch setting, I am living alone and working out my dream or fantasy, which one I do not know. All I do know is that this is how I would love life to be. How this happens I do not know but this is how if possible, it would turn out to be this way. This is why dreaming is so important. You can make life the way you want it to be.

Where passion and desire come from is interesting because they are a part of who we are. What drives us in a direction to certain things and not others? I know people that are passionate about things I cannot understand why. There are those that cannot understand my passion for horses. We all make up a variety of interesting compliments and contradictions. One mans joy is another mans displeasure. We are all unique.

Another passion of mine is children. I was never raised with any children in my family. I do not know where my love for children came from came from but I do know it in my heart. There is enjoyment being around children, talking with them and caring for them. I feel at home in the company of children. It must be the child in me that never grew up as seeing life through the eyes of a child. Everything is simple, not complicated and real. It is too bad that the adults paint a different point of view. We can do children a terrible injustice.

Thinking ahead included having a family with lots of children. A husband that had a good job and we would live happily ever after. The children would be surrounded by joy, fun with life and a desire to achieve to their full potential. The greatest part of dreaming is that I can have this unrealistic view of family life as I see it. This to me would be the ideal.

What I thought was interesting but it never came to a reality. There was anyone who I wanted to marry. It was not that I did not want to but that no one came into my life that I wanted to spend the rest of my life with.

I did pursue one avenue and that was to become a writer. My schooling took me in that direction and by the time college came around, all my classes were geared toward writing. My personal goal is to become a "great" writer. Not so much in recognition but in having an impact on the lives of those who choose to read my books. There is a voice inside of me that is calling out to say to others about what things that I have learned and want to share. Telling stories that would have the reader be involved and have the story surround their lives; Be a part of what is going on inside the book. They are able to act out their involvement in the story. It becomes a part of them.

In pursuing my writing career, I can remember traveling and being compelled to document the things I became involved in and what experiences. Computer technology was not available as it is today. It was a pen and paper in hand which I was comfortable doing. Next it would then be transposed to the typewriter. It seems so old fashioned now because the computer has become my best friend. My life seems to be going in a single style, not with companionship that I am familiar with. I make friends along the way, but I travel and write by myself. It may sound lonely but my mind is constantly thinking and recording information around me. I guess you would say that I am my own best friend.

Not everyone can live like this but the wonderful realization is that they do not have to if they chose differently. Sometimes life turns out that way for a person in a family situation, but this is not the norm. You chose your way and how you get there. I believe that how we embrace circumstances will determine our life and its direction. We make decisions that directly affect our lives. Some of those decisions are uncontrollable but we still have to decide what to do about them. The choices I made were my own.

My Aunt Millie and Uncle Nicks Ranch

So much a part of my life was spending the summers on my aunt and uncles ranch. My uncle was my father's brother and my aunt, of course, was his wife. They were a second family to me and I did embrace them in just that way. Spending time with them and continuing to learn what they knew possibly this is where my passion for horses developed with early intervention having them a part of my life. Growing up with them seemed to have an emotional connection with their spirit. If you can understand this partnership it is a deep connection to the spirit being of something. For me, it is horses and I do understand them in an emotional way. They act and react so many times because of their connection or the experiences they have encountered. It is true that not every horse is the same any more than every child is the same. We touch our inner self with what we can relate to or feel. You know it when you your heart reveals it.

There are people that feel this way about their car, their motorcycle, their boat and much more. They start by giving it a name and the attention they give it. Passion has a quality that will cause many to take it to a level that is out of balance. No matter what the relationship, it cannot consume your life. You have to make room for your family and children unless you are alone and this is what you allow to embrace your life. This being the case, do not take on a wife or have children. If you cannot create the balance then you should not try. Ending up in a family way for whatever reason, you have to relinquish part of that passion for your loved ones. Otherwise there can be consequences that cannot be changed. You can lose what you choose.

The ranch was the epitome of perfection. It had everything I could ever imagine and more. There was so much land that you cannot see from one end to the other. The number of acres is in the 100's. It is located in an area that there are similar ranches in the area. The town is not too far from us because it does border on our property. Considering that the ranch itself is in the middle of the property, we are a distance from town. Not as bad as our neighboring friends. Our trips are few and far between.

The house which is really a home consisting of four bedrooms with a fireplace in each bedroom. The house was built before central heat was a reality, which it is now. The fireplaces were for the purpose of heating the rooms. It sounds unusual now but as a child, I can remember my uncle carrying wood upstairs to my bedroom so I would have heat during the night. The winters were not too cold but we would get snow at the appropriate time of the year. It was never extreme in amount but enough to cause some problems with the running of the ranch.

The tractor was the work horse that never gave up. All you have to do is to fuel it and it would respond. The horses were used for breeding, pleasure and enjoyment. We had so much to do each day it went so fast that you did not realize it.

My aunt did an amazing job of cooking, cleaning and caring for everyone. Her parents were raised in a country that in order to survive, you had to learn how to do everything. Even on the medical side of things, she learned how to take care of most of the situations that would come up. Even stitching a wound was in her capable hands. She learned how to recognize certain plants and herbs that we could use to heal the sick. There were many occasions that her expertise was called upon. Her best feature was her bedside manner. More than her medicine it was the love she expressed in caring for those who needed it. I was the recipient on more than one occasion needing her tender loving care. Her way with taking care of me was as important as the medical treatment.

My uncle was a loving, kind man with so much experience. He and my father had so many stories of their life together and their parents. They were immigrants from Greece and farmers by trade. This is where he developed his passion for horses. His dream was to have a ranch with horses, land and a functioning business making money with the ranch producing its share. The ranch contributed more than its share because he became wealthy starting with one horse, a small home, and a little land.

When he met my aunt, she and her family were in the horse breeding business. They made a wonderful home and business with the two families. My aunt and uncle moved, taking a large sum of money with them to start their own ranch. They were able to purchase all the acres they now own. They built the ranch, stables and barns by themselves. It was a situation that each neighbor would help build your barn and you would help build their barn. The working and sharing relationship was wonderful because they could depend upon each other. They could not have been nearly as successful if it were not for the surrounding ranches.

Once the house was built, then they worked on the barn. They acquired a stud horse for the mare so she could hopefully breed to have a foul. As nature took its course, the mare had her foul in the spring. This was exciting because now there are three. The foul was male so I had the privilege of naming the colt. I named him Lucky Jo. I did not realize that Lucky Jo and I would have such a relationship that would develop over the years. Right now he is a rambunctious colt full of vim, vigor and vitality. He was playful, adorable and completely free to be himself. There were no restrictions on him at the moment because mother is keeping a close eye on him, protecting him, feeding him and watching out for him.

The barn was the next project to be erected. We had a temporary barn for the horses but we needed an adequate structure for more horses. Uncle Nick had plans to breed and stable horses for income and pure joy. He loved what he was doing and what his dream was to become a prominent horse breeder with experience that would be sought after in time. What better combination is there to have than love what you do and make money doing it?

With the completion of the house and barn, we were a functioning ranch. The largest task was to fence off the area of my uncle's property that we wanted to consider the ranch. He had to call in the reinforcements for this task. The property was so vast; it would take a lot of time and man power to complete the job. Fortunately, one of the neighbors had a business that did just such a thing. They had the process of fencing an enormous amount of land by the help of machines. What would take men alone to do cut the time and energy into at least a half. What the machines accomplished took no time at all.

Now that the property is fenced, there was no more worry about the horses getting lost. They could get in trouble but at least they were on the property. He could bring in more horses and capable of handling the job necessary. His goal is becoming a reality and he is happy doing what he loves. It shows in his countenance and in his life. Aunt Millie was happy also because she was able to be what she wanted in life. This is my childhood memory of a wonderful place that was a second home to me. Aunt Millie and Uncle Nick were second parents to me. I loved them both so much.

On the property toward the back is running water cascading and tumbling down over some rocks. The water runs quite rapidly and it is wonderful for swimming. This is where I learned to swim. The refreshing water came from a neighboring lake and this was an outlet for some of the water. It runs throughout the property winding around and even better, there were fish in the water. Learning to fish was a great memory. We had it all and did not realize it when we were younger. As I grew older and my visits had more meaning, appreciation became a part of the experience. It took awhile for the realization that this was an extremely special place and I am so blessed to be a part of it. Being aware that the life that was given me would probably be desired by many. Fortunately, God saw to it that this was the life He wanted for me, Praise the Lord.

The Inheritance

The only child in my father's family, Aunt Millie and Uncle Nick wanted to Will their ranch to me. This came about in later years but as a child I had no idea what this really meant. They felt the relationship we had and the time I spent with them, they wanted me to carry on the legacy they had created. The community depended on them and knowing my passionate love of the ranch, it seemed to be an obvious choice. They had told my father in my early years so my parents were aware of their intentions. No one shared with me that information because at the time, it would have had an overwhelming meaning to me. My thoughts would probably be "How could I ever do this"? The choice to leave their desire quite for the time being was the better decision to make. At this time it did not matter because they were going to live forever. To a young child's perspective, this is rational thinking.

I am now in my thirties, completed college and pursuing my writing career. My decision to travel would bring life to my writing. It is the personal experience which is the best teacher to a writer. The need to feel, respond and react to my environment motivates my writing. My encounter with people brings the story line to a reality. Building my characters from personal information comes from meeting so many wonderful people. The best stories are found in areas that tourists rarely travel. Their lives have so many stories entwined in the lives that are so meaningful and interesting. My choice of characters with emotion helps me identify with them so I can transpose it to paper feeling the person, place and/or thing.

Summers continue spending time with Aunt Millie and Uncle Nick. My parents see me between traveling to places unknown. They are both doing well at this point. My father is getting ready to retire and they have plans to move to Florida where many seniors find their place to live out the retirement years. They love to golf so this is the perfect place for them. My father is a doctor and he can still practice medicine in Florida if he so chooses. Their plans are moving forward and they are anxious to arrive at their new home.

The last summer of my aunt and uncle's life is now a reality. They were driving into town when they met their fate head on with a truck. The truck went out of control and took the car they were in with him. When it finally was able to come to a halt, my aunt and uncle's car was crushed under the wheels. Needless to say, this terrible accident resulted in their death. It was not only unexpected but a tragedy of them losing their life.

The only thing that gave a bit of sunshine to the episode was the fact that they died together which they would have wanted. The terrible result is that with both gone, all the responsibility of the ranch is up to the one who inherits the ranch. At this time, there was no knowledge who this would be. There was no discussion while I was with them. They probably thought they would live a lot longer.

My familiarity with the ranch, all that goes with it and their life was a part of mine. To them, they felt I could step in and take over where they left off. They did not realize that dealing with their death was difficult. Thinking beyond that moment was impossible coping with burying them, making arrangements and deal with the fact they are both gone. The need for help right now came from my parents rescuing me. Depending upon them in time of need is where they always played such an important part.

My parents arrived and we made arrangements. They both wanted to be buried on the property. In fact, they had picked out a place that they both found that they wanted for their final resting place. They did not know that this was going to be prophetic. Their hope became a reality. This is exactly the place we laid them to rest. They will always be a part of this place that they loved. Having their bodies become a part of the soil now is a natural progression of events. I know they would be happy and approve.

We had so much to do plus we had to continue keeping the ranch running. There were things that needed to be done whether we wanted to or not. There was going to be a reading of their Will which we needed to attend. Reluctant to attend but respectfully for them I agreed. I did not want to face the inevitable truth of their death. A Will makes this all so final, even with the burial.

We arrived at the attorney's office and proceeded with the formalities. It was all legal and everything binding. Fortunately, my aunt and uncle did consider having their estate put into finalization upon their death. This was a tremendous benefit for us. It took away any question of the inheritance. The reading of the Will went along in its formal fashion. The thing that took me by surprise is that everything was left to me. My parents knew this was what they desired but it was not until the actual reading of the Will that it became real. This is why they never said anything earlier. This tremendous news leaves me with mixed feelings. My first thought was "How can I ever do this"? This is more than I can cope with at the moment. We left the attorney's office and my parents and I began discussion about what needs to be done.

CHAPTER 2: My Family

Possession of my Inheritance

After the reading of the will, I spent a little more time with my parents. I knew what had to be done but I was questioning my ability to be able to do this. I have to take the ranch and carry on where my aunt and uncle have brought it to this point. They had a functioning ranch and a business to protect. My job ahead of me is huge but I am not alone. My parents asked if I wanted them to stay and I assured them that I would be okay. I just need to get my bearings and I need to know where to begin. They took me at my word and returned to their home. I appreciated their offer to stay but they have a life of their own which is the dream they have set up for their lives. I pray that God will hold them together health wise so they can enjoy their dream as they live it out.

When I was returning from the airport after driving my parents to meet their flight, I had a lot of time to think about the position I am in right now. Now that I have accepted my aunt and uncle's death, I can concentrate on my new family. I turn the corner going up to the ranch house as I cross the bridge. I embrace the view from an entirely different perspective. What was once my aunt and uncle's ranch, my second home, now it is my ranch and my home. I look at the property as I am driving and I realize that all that I see and more is now mine. The dream I had as a child was to have a place like this because I can get in touch with the passion inside of me and live out my dream. Now my dream is a truth and all this belongs to me.

As I view the land from this new perspective as owner not visitor, it has much more meaning. As many times as I have made this drive, it was always their ranch, their property, their possessions and their business. Now there is a new owner who has such a love of this place that making the transformation is actually quite simple. Accepting the responsibility is another story. All I can do is take one day at a time.

As I arrive at the house, I look at it through a different set of eyes. All I see is my aunt and uncle everywhere. I know the first thing I have to do is put me into the ranch. I need to take possession with what I want to surround me. My taste if different than anyone else's and I want to express it in that same way.

I acquire help from a local home improvement center. My desire is to put the colors around that make me feel alive and are conducive to bringing out the writer in me. I have to set up the house the way that brings out the best in me. I have furniture that I have obtained throughout my years of living alone and I need to upgrade the ranch to meet some technical needs. My aunt and uncle saw no need for a computer, cable or any of the new devices available for communication. I was fortunate to be able to have the lines in the area so I can have cable hook up. I am certainly fortunate that those in the surrounding ranches did not object to modern technology. I tried to tell my uncle how the computer would help his business but he could not or did not want to know. He had his own way of doing things. Now that I am alone, I need the technology not only for writing but for keeping track of and running the ranch. Even in the breeding of the horses, the technology will be a great help.

I am now able to have the ranch the way I want it to be. There are certain things that I did not want to change but there are other areas that I needed to reconstruct. I took over my aunt and uncle's bedroom because I wanted the close feeling of them surrounding me. They were happy and the feelings of the home were happy and joyful. I did replace the bed because that was there personal touch with each other. That belongs solely to them. No one deserves their bed but them. I also replace the bedroom furniture with mine because it is what I feel is a part of me. The bedroom itself is beautiful. It is surrounded by windows so the morning light greets you as dawn appears. The fireplaces still work in all the bedrooms but we depend on central heat to warm the house. There is a bay window with a covered bench under the window that you can look out and see so far away. I am on the second floor so the view goes on even farther.

The trees surrounding the house add light and shadows that cast such interesting formations. I am able to set up an area for reading that is off set in the bedroom. The bedroom is large enough to accommodate my queen size bed and my furniture with a little room left over. The closets are more than adequate. When they built the home they had foresight to know that we would need a lot of closet space. The bathroom was right off the bedroom which was to be used only by me. There was another bathroom to accommodate the other two bedrooms. It was a more modern design for the time. There was a back stairway that went directly into the kitchen. The main stairway took you into the bedrooms.

My decorating is completed and when all is said and done, I did a good job discovering me in the home. The bringing together the parts of my aunt and uncle and the parts that are me worked out so well. I redid the kitchen because I won't be cooking like my aunt. I will have help in the kitchen to feed those who are hired to care for the ranch. There is a bunk house that is set up for ranch hands that are there to work the ranch. It is a nice bunk house set up with all the comforts of home. Their only requirement is to keep the place clean and tidy. It is set up with all the necessities to do such a job. There is a washer and dryer for the laundry needs. It is rustic in style but modern in functioning. They even have a microwave in the kitchen. All the responsibilities of the care and keeping of the bunk house are up to them. They do a good job.

Lucky Jo

I have to introduce you to my new family. Each one is such an intricate part of my life; at one time or another they created memories I will never forget. Growing up with them has made them a part of me. They also treat me as such and let me know I am a part of their lives. They are my new family with past experiences that I cherish. Moving in with this environment is like coming home. It is home, real and permanent. I just have to get used to the idea that this is my permanent address.

As I previously described my uncle's first horse, then obtaining a stud horse for the mare. The breeding was successful because when spring arrived so did the foul. It was a healthy male and I had the privilege to name the colt. It was not difficult because Lucky Jo rolled off my tongue. My uncle told me that this was my horse and I would be responsible for him as long as I was there. The months I was away, Lucky Jo would be taken care of as a precious jewel to embrace. He was a gift from God because he fulfilled my dream of having my own horse. It was as if I had given birth to a child of mine. The anticipation and waiting for the coming birth were both exciting and frustration. I wanted him "now" as all children react until maturity takes over. Sometimes that does not happen to some children and then you have a dysfunctional adult. The adult is role playing and looks like an adult but in reality and behavior, they are still a child.

I happened to be on Easter break from school and I made it a point to be on my uncle's ranch at that time. It was time for the mare to birth her foul and I wanted to witness the awesome occasion. I did not realize that it would be such a difficult experience because I was not ready for the pain of birth, the blood, and the inside protection of the foul. All I had ever seen was the baby running around and nursing from mother. I did not realize that birth was so extremely descriptive.

I did arrive for my short stay and I am excited at the prospect of the mare delivering her foul. The time was right but nature still had to take its course. I settled in to my room, enjoyed the conversation with my aunt and uncle and it was as if I had never left. We were always able to pick up where we left off. They were excited about the arrival of the newest family member and the gift they were giving to me. Our expectations were high.

It was early in the evening after dinner when we all settled down for the night. It was a beautiful evening, clear sky, not too chilly and a feeling of spring. The smells in the air are so beautiful. You can pick out different flowers coming into bloom, the grass is coming out of its winter hibernation and the soil was beginning to thaw. You needed a jacket at night and just a shirt during the day.

The sun is the greatest asset to spring or any time of the year. Warming up the atmosphere and having the winter leave and spring to come forward. The sun feels so good after a winter of cold and snow. We never got a lot of snow but enough to balance ecologically nature at its best. The snow is so important to maintaining the growing and planting necessary to support a ranch. It is a wonderful environment and it amazes me that every spring everything starts to grow again. We do not have to speak a word to the trees or grass. They just do as God has commanded them to do when He created their nature. This is there contribution to the necessity of the balance of nature on this earth. God knows everything it needs and accommodates what is necessary. He has perfect solutions to any problem that would arise. He is God Almighty.

As we were settling down Robert, our main ranch hand came to the door to tell us that the mare is ready to deliver. We all grabbed our jackets and ran to the barn. She was down and making terrible noises. These sounds were causing my stomach to upset. I had to get a hold of myself because this was not the time to turn the attention on me. The mare and the foul are the priority. This was their time for us to help if it was necessary. Animals can deliver by themselves and in the wild they do it as a matter of what is natural. They instinctively know what to do. Predators are their greatest concern. So often the birth of an animal will mean food for the other family of wild animals. There is a natural cycle of preservation that is necessary to sustain life in the wild. We do not like to think of it that way but it is a real life scenario.

The mare is struggling and Robert gives the mare the extra help she needs. My uncle is holding her head and comforting her. His gentle voice is soothing to the mare and she feels confident that the situation is going to be alright. It is going through the difficulty of the birth. The foul coming out is painful and stressful. The foul comes out feet first. There is a membrane covering the foul that the mother immediately begins to unwrap her child. The foul struggles while the mother pushes to bring the foul out. All is accomplished and the foul arrives. The foul starts to make sounds and the mother is relieved that her child is alive and well. The mother continues to clean the child and prepares the colt to get on his feet. This is so important that the colt stands up so his lungs can get the air they need. The feat is difficult for the colt but successful. The mare continues to gain her strength so she will be able to nurse the colt.

I watch with amazement as Robert, my uncle and my aunt all participate in this event. We have all been waiting for this moment because my uncle now has three horses and his ranch is beginning to take on the character of a horse breeding ranch. The more horses he can obtain the more successful the business. Of course I could not think of Lucky Jo as a business entity. Lucky Jo was my horse and a fulfillment of the desire of my heart. When he gets older, my uncle can use him to stud. In the meantime he is my horse and I have the job to take care of him and teach him after he is weaned from this mother. He will be about two years old before formal training. Until then, I will raise him as you would a child. I will not forget that he is a horse but the affection and emotion I feel for this horse will develop into a relationship as close as it would be if it were your child.

Kelly

I have not mentioned Kelly but it is time for the introduction. Kelly is my uncle's dog who I first laid eyes on as a puppy. She is a herding dog with inbreed skills at bringing in the horses. Her natural instincts do the job perfectly without human intervention. She is a part of the family and always will be.

I fell in love with her almost immediately. My uncle was given her from a neighboring ranch at his request. He was looking for a dog that could earn its keep by being useful in the running of the ranch. Even though she was a working dog, my uncle fell in love with her as he did all his animals. Not in the sense of physical love but emotional love. He treated them all like family but never crossed the line trying to make them human. He maintained their dignity by keeping them in their natural nature of who they are. Kelly was a dog and loved and respected as such.

One summer when I arrived at the ranch, I was introduced to Kelly. At that time, she was about 3 months old and as cute and frisky as a pup would be. She would get into trouble which she was supposed to do. She would cause problems with the horses, not knowing that her job was going to be to help take care of them. But for now, she wanted to play and pester them. She was annoying to them but to me she was fantastic.

She reached a level of intelligence early in her young life. She was obedient upon command but full of mischief when she could get away with it. She slept in the house but certainly not a furniture dog. My aunt and uncle would not allow it. As she matured, she would spend nights in the barn with a troubled horse just to comfort and be a companion. She was happy and enjoyed life to the fullest. As she roamed the ranch, she discovered all the wonderful mysteries to be discovered.

I remember one time, we were missing Kelly. It was a situation she would go out to explore and would be gone for a while. There was nothing to be concerned with at the time. We became aware of her absence and we began to be concerned. It is one of those situations that just do not feel right. We began our search in the obvious places and then extended that search to places that she may need help. Our anxiety began rising as we were not able to find her. I will not say we panicked but we were more than concerned.

Our search led us to an area that we were in the process of redesigning for the purpose of the horses. It was to be a breeding barn to assist the horses and a place that they can deliver their fouls. while building the barn, my uncle discovered an old cave that had been abandoned. It was constructed probably many years ago for mining. It was concealed by the hills that have taken over its presence. Over growth, brush and trees were its covering. They were using the hills as a background for the barn to have it out of the way for privacy. The horses could be alone at the times they needed to be in order to do what was necessary at the time.

    As we approached this area, we could hear sounds of whimpering and struggle. We immediately began overturning what we had to in order to discover where the sounds were coming from. We thought it was Kelly so we furiously began digging into the rubble to find her. The next few minutes were agonizing as she continued to make sounds to bring us to her. She could not bark so the whimper was the best we had.

    We reached her and she was buried under some stone and rock. Fortunately, the largest ones missed her. I could see her brown and white coat which was almost unrecognizable with the dirt and debris. I could see some blood coming from her leg. She was almost unconscious but held enough strength within her battered body to bring us to her. When we arrived to rescue her, she went into unconsciousness; she knew she was safe. We are there to take her home.

    We gathered her wounded body, put her in the wagon we brought with us, in order to get her home. We could call the Vet and he could come and take care of her. A Veterinarian in this area had to make house calls because livestock is difficult to transport. In this case, Kelly was too badly injured and should not be moved. We thought she had a broken leg but the unconscious state was such a concern.

The Vet arrived quickly and made an assessment of her condition. It seems that her being unconscious was a good thing. She could rest her body. It is normal under the circumstances that the falling rock gave her a minor concussion. A concussion is because of the blow. If it were a fracture, it would be much more serious. As the Vet continued to examine her, he did conclude she did have a broken leg. The blood was from a superficial wound and was not serious. He could take care of that easy enough. He set her leg; we cleaned her up, and waited for her to return to consciousness. She began to come around and she was so happy to see us. Her last recollection was in the cave whining for our help. She did not realize until now that she was rescued.

Animals and children have such resilience to their situations and an uncanny way of dealing with their pain. They adapt so well to the needs of their bodies that the wound becomes a part of them. Kelly was just this way. After a day or two of rest, she was up and around with a splint on her leg. She favored the leg so she would not injure it more. She knew enough not to put any pressure on it. A three-legged dog was perfectly capable of taking care of itself. We, of course, had no demands on her but she voluntarily began to step up to the plate. She wanted to continue to work.

While Kelly was recuperating, she spent a lot of time in the stall with Lucky Jo. I did not realize that they were developing such a close relationship. As I was thinking back, I remember seeing them together a lot. In fact, whenever I was riding Lucky Jo, Kelly was right there. I do know that animals will turn to each other for emotional support. It was exciting to me because both of them are so dear to my heart.

In fact, Kelly got to the point that she wanted to sleep in the barn with Lucky Jo. Kelly had the freedom to choose because my aunt and uncle never wanted to control Kelly. She was a working dog and staying in the barn was appropriate. What we did not realize was that she always chooses to stay with Lucky Jo.

Fudzer

Fudzer is the cat that has become a part of my life. The name may seem unusual but a neighbor's child saw our little black and white kitten and in her childish language she could not say fuzzy. It came out Fudzer. We thought it was adorable so Fudzer it was. She came to the ranch via our neighbor who knew my uncle was looking for a cat. Our expectations were that she would keep the mice away and any critters that decided to make our ranch their home. This was not going to be an option, so Fudzer became a part of the family.

As with Kelly, Fudzer could come into the house but she had to behave as a cat and not a person. She was expected to stay on the floor and not the furniture. Because she had the rule and rein of the outdoors, she did not need to scratch the furniture or be up with the adults. She learned very early that her place was a cat and was expected to be a cat. We were not about to make her into a person. Her beauty is her cat characteristics.

This is where she begins to shine. As a kitten, she was funny, pleasant and adorable. She did get into mischief but it was childlike. That was part of her charm. She could find any number of things to play with to keep her amused. We made certain things available for her to challenge in a duel. She did not always win.

One of the things I remember about her was the day she went outside for her daily routine of stalking out the ranch. She was about six months old by now and her natural instincts are taking over. Her role as mouse catcher she is taking very serious. Somehow my uncle was able to convey to her that she was to keep the mice out of the barn. They were upsetting the horses. In her first attempt at being the great protector of the barn, she did succeed in catching that pesky mouse that was terrorizing the horses. You would not think a horse the size they are would react to a mouse. It was their quickness and ability to move so fast that made the horses nervous. The mouse can easily go from one stall to another. There seemed to be no boundaries as far as the mouse was concerned.

The first time she was successful was a mixed blessing. She knew her duty was to keep the mice out of the barn. This was one of her jobs. On this particular morning she was scaling her territory when she spotted a mouse. This mouse was seen often and a nuisance to the calmness of the barn. The mouse showed up and the horses did respond. They did not like it. In her ability to hunt and stalk, Fudzer found a way to corner the mouse and she was successful. The mouse is history. She was so proud of herself because she knew she did what my uncle wanted and expected of her. What my uncle did not know was that she thought this mouse was a trophy and brought the dead mouse to him. In his momentary surprise and amazement, he realized what Fudzer had done. He showed her he was proud of her accomplishment and then took her outside to show her where to deposit her hunt. She is such a quick learner that this was the only time she brought him a dead mouse. She did continue to take the remains of the dead mice to the appropriate place.

While her presence was quite obvious, Kelly was not sure at first about this fuzzy thing that wanted to play and annoy her. Kelly was not a jealous dog but she could not control Fudzer as a kitten. Kelly spent a lot of time watching out for the kitten but was not too sure about getting involved. One day while Fudzer was on her barn duties, she decided to go into a dark area to see if she could scare out a mouse or two. In her investigative skills she found herself trapped between some sort of tool and refuge from the field. It must be storage for something but it certainly had Fudzer trapped. In her fright, she began to squeal, and thrash, but it could ultimately harm her. Her desperation was obvious and Kelly could hear her and then sees what the problem was. Instinctively, Kelly began looking for a way out for the cat, trying to save her. As Kelly barked, Fudzer knew Kelly was there to rescue her. Fudzer settled down and let Kelly do her work. Kelly could see the problem and proceeded to free the cat. As Fudzer was able to get free, she came out and Kelly began licking her. Fudzer was grateful and responsive. She knew she had a soul mate that would protect her from now on. After that incident, Kelly took to Fudzer as a mother would protect her own. They had bonded and now inseparable.

Once Kelly had adopted Fudzer, she took Fudzer in the stall with Lucky Jo. Lucky Jo was familiar with Fudzer because she was the one that got rid of those mice. Lucky Jo would watch as Fudzer took care of him. As Fudzer follows Kelly into Lucky Jo's stall, there was an immediate reaction of acceptance. Fudzer would rub against Lucky Jo's leg. Believe it or not, when Fudzer got bigger and could jump up on things, she challenged herself to the edge of the stall and managed to get on the back of Lucky Jo. When we witnessed this, we were astonished with disbelief. The greater mystery was that Lucky Jo did not mind. Kelly at the feet of Lucky Jo and Fudzer on the back of Lucky Jo and the three were an unlikely team. What makes animals choose one another is not known but this unlikely trio was bonded for life.

Robert

To describe Robert think of Robert Redford in "The Horse Whisperer". This description of his appearance does describe Robert but the difference is that his life was nothing like that. His story goes back to when my uncle first began the ranch, purchased the property and began to build the house and barn.

One day while my uncle was in town getting supplies, he heard of a man looking for work and a place to stay. His life story is a tragedy which changed him forever. His entire family lost their life to a fire that ultimately took everything Robert owned. He was devastated and destitute and began wondering aimlessly to find his way to somewhere but he did not know where that would be. His reputation was that he was quite, did not want trouble from anyone and trustworthy. His personality was half destroyed by the loss of his family. He was half alive emotionally. He was a good worker and needed the work. My uncle had a good sense of character and was good at knowing people. He met Robert and as it turned out, they bonded for life. The life of my uncle and now he was there for me.

While growing up, I loved spending time with Robert. I know he liked me just the way he acted with me. He did not talk about his family but he did say one time that I reminded him of his daughter. As a child I could not learn enough. Robert and my uncle were so good to me with all the "whys" and "how comes" that came out of my mouth. They used to get a kick out of me and my perception of life; especially when it came to the animals.

CHAPTER 3: The River

Enjoying its Beauty

The beauty of the land is unbelievable but its assets are incredible. In the back of the property ran a river which you could hear as you approach the area. The sound of running water and the feel of its changing temperature as the mist crosses through the air is so exciting and refreshing. God created everything and water was certainly a part of that. The running water coming from the mountains and above the present elevation is poetic, entrancing and exciting to behold. The way it continually moves and never stops; changing its shape continually as it tumbles over the underlying rocks. This cascade of falling, moving water can be overpowering if you should get in its path. The density of the water depends upon the time of year. Spring always brings the greatest amount when the snow in the mountains begins to melt. I can see the mountains from our property but the actual distance is quite a way from us. Fortunately for us, the river runs through my uncle's property and finds its way to a neighboring lake.

I can remember riding back to the waterfalls just to absorb its beauty. The symphonic repetition of sounds created a melody that portrayed music to me. I would close my eyes, feel the moist air, and listen to what the river was telling me. I was feeling a sensation of being one with the water as if I understood what it was saying. It was a welcoming response because the river knew I was not a threat and was embracing what it was.

I know the river is not a person but God created nature in its beauty and what God has created is beautiful. My emotions and imagination are capable of making anything I want to become what I want. This is why we should cherish our minds. They can be the private place that you and the Lord inhabit and no one can change what you are thinking or feeling. This is truly a gift from God. We have to keep our mind healthy and in tune to God so that this playground is not inhabited for anything but good. You can create anything you want in your mind and God wants that to be for good.

Swimming and Diving

Farther down stream, there was an area that we could swim. The water was still in motion, but it was moving just enough that we could have fun. I do not remember learning how to swim so it must have been when I was quite young. I learned to be respectful of the water but I also learned how much fun it was to play in. I was a fish, a water animal and even a person. There were fish in the water and it was fun swimming after them. Of course, I never caught one by hand and actually I never really wanted to. The pursuit was the adventure.

There were days that I would swim for hours. I would have Lucky Jo, Kelly, and Fudzer with me to enjoy the water. Lucky Jo would come in the water and let me ride him bareback. We had more fun going back and forth in the water. With the changing depths, we could go from me being uncovered from the water to being submerged with him. I would hold onto his mane and he would try to swish me off. We played this game and I must admit I did not win very often. He was not only smart but quick to respond. The water hindered me more than him.

On the edge of the river, above the water, there was an area that over looked the river. Lucky Jo and I would go up to it and then we would jump off together; I was on his back and I could make those sounds like the cowboys and Indians would do. At least I thought they did.

Kelly was a typical dog around the water. She loved to swim, chase things I would throw for her in the water and she also jumped off our platform with us. She loved chasing the fish, the surrounding creatures as they would scamper from her threat. She had the rule and rein over the area because anything living around there knew enough to hide.

The presence of Fudzer certainly gave the surrounding creatures a reason to get out of sight. Her quick instinct, her ability to move and patient to wait was her asset. Her reputation with mice must have gotten the word out to the surrounding inhabitants because when she showed up, they evacuated. Kelly was not as much of a threat because she would rather bark and play with them. Fudzer was another story. She was the great hunter and they were the prize. Instinctively they knew that and they had met their match.

Fudzer was not much for the swimming but involved in our fun. She was on the river bank, I would splash and she would turn tail and run. She would cautiously come back, and again, play the game. She had more fun watching and playing than participate in our water games. Her joy was just being a cat and doing what she loved. Being with us was fulfillment enough and finding her present sense of pleasure; much like children. They can invent joy with nothing. It is part of their marvelous nature.

Fishing

A memory I cherish is one that my uncle and I would share. We would go down to the river and we would fish. He had such a knack at finding fish and bringing them in. He knew how to get the job done. His sense of timing and his patience were his greatest asset. I would observe him in action and I learned so much.

We did not have fancy gear, but it certainly did the work of catching the fish. We chose worms for our bait, a small hook and light line. The sizes of the fish were surprisingly large for this habitat. It was probably because the river was not fished often and they had a chance to grow.

My uncle taught me to cast out, retrieve slowly to let the fish follow my bait and we were successful fishermen. The anticipation was exciting but the time we spent together, talked and enjoyed each others company was the best part. We would have fish for dinner. My aunt thought that was the best part. Home grown fish cooked in her oven. She did make my uncle clean them. Thankfully it was not me because I know I could not have caught fish, cleaned them and then had them for dinner. I had to forget the middle part. That would have been too much. I am so happy my uncle agreed with me.

One day we were fishing and I remember a story my uncle told me about an Indian who lives back on the property with his family. When my uncle bought the land they were already settlers there and had made a home for themselves. The previous owners did request that they still live there if it was possible. As the story went, the Indian family rescued my uncle several times when the need arose. My uncle felt they deserved to stay there and as it turned out they became a distant part of the family. They did stay to themselves but ironically, they would show up in a time of need. I do not believe that was coincidence. I believe it was divine intervention.

The first time my uncle met the Indian was while fishing. He spoke English which was good. He learned from some missionaries that taught his ancestors and passed it down to them. Where they did live was close to the reservation which did border my uncle's property on the

South side. The property they built their home on off the river bank down stream and then into a neighboring lake. They could live off of the land.

When they met the Indian we called Chief, thanked my uncle for letting he and his family stay on his property. While they were fishing they began telling stories and Chief related many situations that brought history to the property. It was fascinating to be a part of this. He noticed how my uncle began to transform the property into a ranch. Chief has a few horses of his own so they could share their passion for horses.

One day while they were fishing my uncle got up to get some more bait. He turned to reach for his stash of worms when he slipped on the wet mud, took a tumble and hit his head on a rock. The momentum threw this body forward and he went head on into the river. The water was running quite rapidly because of the spring thaw. There was evidence of blood as my uncle hit the water and it washed his head. He was unconscious but moving with the water. Chief immediately jumped to his feet, and struggled to grab my uncles flowing body. His first attempt was unsuccessful but as he followed his body down stream, Chief sought the opportunity to retrieve my uncle. He was successful at stopping his body from going any farther. With some difficulty, Chief was able to pull his body from the water and rest him on the river bank. My uncle was unconscious with the head wound. As chief examined him, he thought he would be alright but he went for help. He made my uncle as comfortable as possible. They were closer to Chiefs home so he ran to what he needed to help my uncle.

Upon his return, his wife Tamar and a wagon arrived so they could transport my uncle back to the ranch. Chief knew my uncle would get help there or the doctor would come. My uncle still unconscious, they did bring him to the ranch and they were able to care for him. Chief and his wife stayed to see if he was alright. My uncle regained consciousness and could not thank Chief enough for saving his life. This bond continued all their lives.

Canoeing

Another talent that my uncle had to attribute to Chief is that he taught him how to canoe. Canoeing seems simple enough but has so many obstacles, this one was challenging. Chief was practically born in a canoe so to us, it was more difficult. My uncle was a good learner but nothing compared to Chief. What my uncle did learn was enough that he and I could have a great time canoeing down the river. One of the first requirements is that you realize that when you go down river you have to return up river. Either you paddle hard at first, go upstream, and then coast down or visa-versa. The smart way is to go upstream and the coast down. Sometimes we would get a ride from Robert's truck. He would put the canoe on the bed of the truck, drive us upstream, and we would canoe back. That was great and a lot of fun; much easier than canoeing up but not as rewarding as the struggle. My uncle liked the struggle and then the reward. I think I did too because we had to really work together.

One day we decided to make the trip upstream and then come back to the ranch. It was a beautiful day but the previous night was quite an event. Thunder and lightening were everywhere and the sound and fury were pretty frightening Fortunately my uncle's barn is grounded so lightening would not strike the barn but the animals did not know that. We endured the night only to experience a marvelous sunrise. The experience of the anger and rage in the sky that night and now the beauty of the morning is amazing. There is victory as the moist air is refreshed as the sun begins to warm the air around us. The animals know it is over but it did take awhile to bring them to a peaceful demeanor. As we proceeded to take that canoe trip upstream we were definitely challenged by the debris of the storm the night before. It was a summer storm so the air was pleasant but the canoeing was difficult. We made headway but obstacles seemed to control our path. The journey was difficult enough going upstream let alone maneuvering around fallen trees and branches. Much of the night's fury disrupted the growth on the river bank. We managed for quite awhile and then all of the sudden our canoe abruptly turned with the running water, we went sideways into a fallen branch and over we go. I knew enough to stay with the canoe and so did my uncle. As we surfaced from the overturn, we held on tight to the canoe. The water was not so deep but finding a place we could stop and gain control of ourselves and the canoe was difficult. Our paddles went ahead of us, as well as the lunch my aunt packed for us. We stayed with the moving canoe until we had an option. We did not know what that was but we would recognize it when it came our way.

To our amazement we saw Lucky Jo and Kelly in the distance. They must have followed us as they did often; probably wanting to keep an eye on us and partly to be a part of the adventure. Regardless of the reason, they were coming to our rescue.

Tangled in debris, caught by a fallen branch and the water moving we were in a situation we could not help ourselves. We knew to stay with the canoe but we were stuck to where we could not get free. We needed help and soon. When Lucky Jo and Kelly arrived, they were anxious and did not know what to do. Fortunately, Lucky Jo had on his harness which was a possibility to help us.

. We commanded Kelly to try to get the harness as Lucky Jo would bend his neck so she could get a hold of it. She was able to get the harness and she walked out the fallen branch to give the harness to us. I being the smaller of the two of us, I was elected to grab the harness. Kelly bravely and cautiously maneuvered across the branch with the harness in her mouth. Lucky Jo would hold fast so Kelly would have a little grip crossing the branch. I was able to grab a hold of the harness, Lucky Jo back up so I could get my bearings. The taunt rein gave me leverage and I was able to make it to the shoreline and Lucky Jo could help pull me up. I was exhausted from being pushed against the debris.

My uncle experiencing the same thing anxiously awaited for me to help rescue him. I was able to get to my feet and Kelly proceeded to take the rein to my uncle. She repeated the performance, my uncle was able to get free, and between the three of us, my uncle made it to the shoreline also. He being older, needed a little more time to rest. Lucky Jo and Kelly were so happy they could rescue us; they would dance and prance to show their pleasure. Of course, we responded with the appropriate gestures of hugs and kisses. We were wet, tired but so thankful that our family knew enough to follow us and be there to meet our need.

As the canoe continued floating down stream we figured we would probably catch up to it at the place we put in. Canoes won't sink so we could retrieve it if it is not damaged. We would know when we find it. Lucky Jo let us on his back and we proceeded home. With Kelly at our side, the trip home gave to us a sense of pride in the animals and a fortunate feeling that they were capable of rescuing us. I know the Lord had His hand in this because He was watching out for us. He was able to use Lucky Jo and Kelly to be the blessing we needed. Thank You, Lord.

CHAPTER 4: The Inhabitants of the Property

The Indian Family

Part of the landscape and the aesthetics of the property are the inhabitants who are permanent residence living there for a long time. Chief and his family have been dwellers here for years. There was much to be learned from them and they could learn from us. I can remember my own personal experiences with the family. In fact, I grew up with the children while I was here living with my aunt and uncle.

I remember the time that I was at the river swimming with Lucky Jo and Kelly. Fudzer was tagging alone but having as much fun. She was absorbed in her own world as we were in ours. I thought I was alone when in the distance I could see a boy and a girl of Indian decent. I knew the family lived there and my uncle shared many affectionate stories with them involved. I felt I knew them by description and by the intimate relationship between Chief and my uncle. The children and Chief's wife Tamar I knew only by information given by my uncle.

I saw them coming and as I observed they had their horses also. A beautiful paint and a gorgeous black stallion; the painted horse belonged to the girl and the black was the boys. Lucky Jo was a chestnut quarter horse and a gentlemen but capable of defending himself and us also. Seeing the other horses he knew he should be cautious but he did sense there was no danger. He observed as the boy and girl approached and did not rest easy until we spoke. They were so nice and friendly that it was clear that they just wanted to have fun with us. Their names were Princess (a nickname) and Ahoe, meaning "strong one" in their language. I was fascinated by what I could learn from them but right now it was time to play.

We, Lucky Jo and Kelly, would do our "Swish" in the water and jump off the ledge we had done so many times before. The horses were having a great time playing as we were. Children have an uncanny way of making friends without reservation as the adult world does. It did not matter to us who they were just that they were having as much fun as us. They did have a dog accompany them so Kelly had someone to challenge and play with. Being that it was a male dog, I think there was more there than met the eye. It did turn out that Ranger, the dogs name, did accommodate Kelly and father her litter, but that is another story.

After our time of swimming and doing what kids and animals do, I invited both Princess and Ahoe to the ranch to meet the others. They knew of my uncle and aunt but they saw Robert often but had never really met him. As it turned out, the Black Stallion was a perfect stud horse for the mares. We were able to work out an arrangement with Chief so we would both benefit. This new relationship helped both of us increase our herd of horses.

A long time ago, my uncle decided that they would make Lucky Jo Gilding, which means to neuter him so he would not want to stud. Being that he was "MY HORSE", my uncle wanted to keep him tame for me. Once Lucky Jo reached the maturity to want to stud, they did what they had to do to keep him from being a wild male horse. He just was not interested in the mares after that and he was the best companion. I am so pleased that my uncle had the foresight to do this so I could raise him as my pet and keep him calm and a perfect companion.

Chief and his wife invited us to their camp. They were interested in us as well as we were interested in them. I wanted to know all about their culture, what they thought about things and how they lived. Living on the border of the reservation, they were schooled and receive assistance from the tribe. They enjoyed being able to continue living on our property as was the agreement of the previous land owner. We were the fortunate ones having them as friends and neighbors. On so many occasions they not only rescued us but taught us so much about living in the wild. Our property was civilized but many obstacles were a part of the land. I learned more than enough to survive in the open if I ever needed the knowledge.

I can remember talking to and watching Chief's wife, Tamar, cook and clean the meat they would kill on the Reservation. There were deer, rabbits and other animals they would eat but we probably would not but I guess it is all how you are raised. They would eat snake and would know which ones were edible. I am glad we did not eat that but the Indians considered it a meal. They did not hesitate.

They grew corn and other vegetable. They had an abundance of squash, pumpkin and potatoes. They had access to some fruit trees which helped to supplement their diet. We brought a Bull and a few cows to them so they could have milk and taught them about the meat from the cow. They learned from us and we learned from them. Our contribution to help them and the people on the reservation gave them a good quality of life.

We were dependent on each other but we all were rewarded for the relationship. I especially loved the opportunity to learn about another culture and have friends to spend time with. Being that I was an only child on the ranch, Princess and Ahoe were my best friends. Our adventures we would make up as we would go along are embedded in my mind forever. Chief and Tamar were like parents to me and they enjoyed learning about the things in my life when I was not there and with my parents.

The Animals of the Environment

I have revealed some of the creatures who we have made their home on our property. They were here first until we decided to make this our home. Actually we are the aliens and strangers to the land. Animals have no control over the desires of what they want or where they live. They instinctively settle in places they feel will be safe and supply their need for food. Human Beings often designate that by wanting what they already have. We see it, we want it and we either take it or purchase it. Animals have no defense in their ability to stop any of this. All we do is kill the animals that are in our way. If the need for food is the priority, that is what God has provided for us to survive. But if it is just malicious intent, it is cruel and sin against God. We are to take care of the animals God has given us.

There is the balance of nature which is God's design. Some live because others have died. But when it is a means of destroying something just for the sake of the kill or to see the animal die or suffer, this is wrong. We will be held responsible before God for our actions. God looks at the intentions of the heart and if we disrespect one of His own, we are guilty of murder. You may say, "It is only an animal" but God reveres His creation with a Holy intent. If we do wrong to an animal, is a human being next?

As the weather begins to take on the chill of winter, the deer seem to come closer to the ranch for food. We have made it possible for the deer to have food which we planted early in the season. With an abundance of food available they stay away from our crops which we need for the winter months.

I remember one time when Lucky Jo, Kelly and I were out and about doing what we do best, explore. We were on a great adventure of who knows what when we spotted a fawn in the distance. Logically thinking in my mind was that the mother deer would be close by. As I scanned the area with my eyes, I could not see her. There were trees and brush camouflaging the area but the fawn was visible. As we slowly approached, the fawn became nervous. She probably did not know what we were or what to expect. Her natural instinct would be to run and hide but she intended to stay close. She did not run but she did react in a fearful way. I instinctively knew something was wrong. Our approach was cautious, but I could see that the mother was caught in the thicket, entangled to where she could not move. She made sounds of fear and was troubled for her fawn. The fawn stayed close to her but was afraid of us.

    I dismounted Lucky Jo and spoke softly to Kelly. She knew there was trouble and understood the position we were to play. She contained her barking so the fawn and mother would not react with more fear than they were already experiencing. As I approached the tangled deer, I used my voice to try to reassure her. I could see why she could not move to free herself. Her leg was bleeding and the thistle had her pinned down.

    I motioned for Lucky Jo to come closer. Believe it or not, Kelly stayed with the fawn to reassure her. The fawn could feel the comfort she was there to give her. The mother was in danger and the fawn new this. The fawn could feel that we were there to help.

    As I used my voice and had Lucky Jo come closer, I could use the reins to pull some of the entangled debris away. Lucky Jo knew what my intention was and assisted when he could. Pulling and tugging was the best option. Our persistence paid off because we could free the deer. She struggled to her feet but she did favor the caught leg. Her struggling to free herself did complicate the capture but her fear for her fawn was overpowering. Examining her wound we could determine how bad it was injured. She did not choose to run or attempt to run. She allowed us to help her.

I found some appropriate supports for her leg and I happened to have a scarf I decided to put on last minute. It must have been Divine intervention again but God knew we would need that scarf for a bandage. I learned from my Indian family how to use certain greens available for antiseptic. In my search I did find what I needed. The mother deer and the fawn were bonding showing each other the relief of her freedom. The fawn examined the wound and instinctively knew it had to be fixed.

Upon returning, the deer waited for the next move. She let me close to her so I could dress the wound. I wrapped the wound with the leaves I found, added the supports for the leg, and then wrapped both with the scarf. I needed enough pressure to hold the brace secure but not too much that would cause more pain to the deer. I was "Dr. Mom" for the moment and the deer was relieved. She was able to limp on that leg but tried not to favor it too much. Instinctively she knew she had to take care of herself for her fawn. The fawn was still nursing from her mother so her well-being was so important for the survival of the fawn.

The deer made her way into the trees and the fawn followed. The fawn turned for a precious look that said it all. I thought in my mind, "You're welcome". We knew that the mother would be able to free herself from her bandages when the leg was sufficiently healed.

On our journeys as we would explore, I would keep an eye out for them but I never did see them again. I do know they are safe from the human factor; there was no hunting on our property. If they did wonder over to the reservation, they may have met their destiny and become the food that the Indians needed to live. This is that balance of nature that is played out in order to survive.

There were rabbits, chipmunks, squirrels, and water creatures. There were ducks when the water was not running too fast, but they enjoyed the lake more. We had beaver also but the problem was that they would want to dam up the river and we needed it to run free. It would seem that every spring we would have to help relocate the winter inhabitants. We did find an off area where the river would take a turn and the beaver could do what comes naturally to them. They could build until they did not want to build anymore. We were able to help encourage the beaver to choose this particular area after we were able to determine their strategy. Much like people we wanted them to think it was their idea. If you learn to observe, you can learn to communicate with the animals without coming into direct contact with them. This is how man and animal have learned to survive with each other, keeping a respect for each others domain.

The worst inhabitants to the property were a pack of wild dogs. They were fine as long as they stayed where we were not. Occasionally they would try to approach the area fenced off which is what we considered the ranch. My uncle had more property but there was a certain amount he designated for the ranch and its needs. The dogs did not inhabit the civilized area but they were a constant threat. You could expect them to make themselves known if they were looking for food or other means of survival. As a pack they work together and look out for one another. They are territorial but as a family unit, they do stick together.

They can jump a fence if it is not too high. At times they would make their way through a distant part of the fencing and they were through it before we realized it. My uncle is not a hunter by nature but he had to kill the dogs if they did come near. You could not reason with them or try to be friendly. They did not care or they did not want to. The only course of action was to arm yourself with a rifle and be forced to use it if it became necessary. A life threatening situation to any of the animals or any person was reason enough. The wild nature they portrayed made me realize they were not pets. I did not like the fact that they might have to be shot but I did understand there really was no choice.

One day Lucky Jo, Kelly and I went on a ride, packed a lunch and decided we would ride the perimeter of the property. This meant a day of exploring, riding and creating an adventure. We had done this before and I loved it because you could enjoy the surroundings so much; that is where I came into a situation like saving the mother dear and rescuing her. You often have to put yourself out there so you can help someone or something that needs help.

It was a beautiful day; the temperature was perfect for riding with a jacket being all you needed. The smell in the air was fresh and clean. It smelled of grass, greens and trees. I love this smell because it always reminds me of the creation of God, perfect. He knew what to put together when He created the earth to keep it all in balance. The right trees that help other trees grow the right grass to feed the animals and of course, the clean water that flows from the mountains. This is beauty to perfection and purpose. All of this contributes to the balance of nature.

We must have been approximately an hour into our ride when Kelly took off running. This usually meant she found something to play with and antagonize or something was wrong. Lucky Jo and I put it into gear and we followed. Kelly was running so fast we had to break into a canter. As we neared her destination we came to a halt to observe what

Kelly had in mind and to see if we could determine what was going on. We could hear some yelping sounds and Kelly was standing by an area that had piles of dirt surrounding the area. She started barking to make us aware of what she found. As we got there, we could see that there had been some digging. My first thought was a hole which was dug. I know my uncle and Robert were out doing some fencing which did entail digging. Possibly this was the area. They covered the area to make it safe so none of the animals would be trapped in the hole. I do know the storm two nights ago had strong wind and possibly enough force to release the cover over the hole. This could be what had happened.

I could still hear the whelping and Kelly continued to bark. As I got close to the hole, I could see a frightened wild dog pup trapped inside. He could hardly move. The hole was approximately six feet deep and impossible for the pup to get out. He looked alright as far as any wound may be present, but his fear was obvious. This, of course, is expected.

This being a wild pup, he probably did not know who or what we were. Kelly could make the pup feel threatened or more comfortable depending upon his nature. I would rather believe that Kelly made the pup feel more secure being from the same animal family. Regardless, this was going to be difficult because I am not sure I can get the pups cooperation.

Whenever we take one of these trips, we do take some survival equipment besides food. A rope, a knife, a few tools, a blanket and some first aid supplies. This is for precautions sake. I learned early from my uncle that you should always be prepared in case of an emergency. If you were to take a trip by car, you do not expect something to happen but if it does, you want to be able to help yourself. Anytime you leave home you want to be prepared.

My first thought was to offer the pup something to eat. I do not know how long the pup has been trapped, but food could be a friendly gesture and a good one if he is hungry. I could feel a sense of anxiety because I knew the mother and possibly the pack would or could be close looking for the pup. I knew they were close in the area. They would be quiet in order to seek out the pup if it were in danger. They would not know immediately if we were a threat or not.

The pup accepted the peace offering, and was hungry. I thought if I could send some water down, he would not only need a drink but would recognize we were helping and wanted to get him free. I took a piece of cloth, tied it to the end of the rope, and gently lowered it down. It was wet enough with water dripping off the end that the pup could get a drink. He even put the cloth in his mouth as if to suck out the water. His demeanor was calming and I believe he began to understand that we wanted to help him in this helpless situation he was in. I retrieved the rope and figured that if I could somehow get the rope around the pup, Lucky Jo could pull the pup out. I tried to tell the pup what we were doing. I do not know if it was the words or the sound of my voice that seemed to calm the pup. Trust was beginning to bind us together. I saw the pup seemed ready to cooperate.

I am lying upon the piled dirt, beginning to lower the looped rope to see if I could lasso the pup and get the rope around his center so that when we got to lift him out of the hole, the circled rope will slide forward and position itself around his front legs. This would make it easier because he would then become elongated and easier to bring out of the hole. There was very little room to maneuver.

As I am making several attempts to get this loop around the pup, he was very cooperative. I am concentrating on rescuing this pup. All of the sudden Kelly started barking anxiously and quite intently. This caused the pup to become upset and struggle to get out again. My first reaction was to yell at Kelly when Lucky Jo began to become unsettled, whinny and nay. I turned to look and my heart skipped a beat. Approaching us, growling and barking were the pup's family. We were threatened and fearful because the pack did not know what we were doing. All they could hear was the pup in trouble. I tried to calm Lucky Jo and Kelly but I was scared and did not know what to do. The pack continued to come closer, growling and threatening. I thought that if they could see the pup in peril, they possibly would understand we were there to help. How could they understand the human response to a human resolution?

    I backed away from the opening so the pack could observe the pup in the hole. They needed to see the pup was alright but trapped. I really believed they would understand we were there to help the pup, not hurt him. This was the only thing I could think of at the moment. I was trying to think like the wild dogs and what would help them to understand we were not the threat. We were the answer to the problem. As I moved away and let the dogs observe the pup, there was barking from both. The pack and the pup were communicating. I cannot read dog language but somehow the pup was able to help the pack realize that we were there to help. It was amazing because they cautiously backed away so we could continue. Kelly and Lucky Jo held themselves for the moment because the dogs had released their attacking attitude, backed off, and let us continue. Believe me, I was more nervous than before but I had to focus on the pup. If anything happened to the pup, I did not know what would happen.

I had to calm down the pup again. It was a bit easier because he felt secure with his family there to protect him. I still needed to get this rope around his belly so we could pull him up. After several tries, Kelly was able to help me place the rope in the proper position. Lucky Jo was ready to bring him up. The rope did exactly what it was suppose to and the pup arrives at the surface. I grabbed the rope to bring the pup to safety. I was able to take the rope off the pup and turn him over to his family. It was a typical family reunion. It was a symphony of licks and happy barks and relieved that one of their own was safe and secure. We were happy to see their joy. We felt good about the fact we could save the pup.

Now the moment of truth has come to our awkward, difficult situation. There was still the matter we had to cope with the dogs. Lucky Jo, Kelly and I turned our attention on re-covering the hole so nothing else would fall into it again. The first thing was to cover the opening and then secure it with the wood that was to hold the covering down. Some properly positioned rocks did the trick. This would be good until we could get back to the ranch and tell my uncle what happened and he would see to correcting the situation.

The dogs were quietly observing what we were doing. I know they could sense we were not a threat and even thankful for what we had done. I turned to the leader of the pack and approached him with a sense of offering myself in a friendship response. I looked him straight in the eyes as if to say your welcome. We were communicating and I wanted to see if the pup was alright or not. I did not know if the leader would let me close to the pup, let alone the pup's mother. As I used my voice to say words they did not understand but did understand a friendly voice. I started to go to the pup and both the leader and the mother let me look at the pup. Other than covered with dirt, the pup was fine. He even licked my hand to say thank you. I backed away still facing them, they turned to go on their way and disappeared into the trees. I felt a sense of relief for so many reasons but my feeling for the animal kingdom just escalated a couple of notches. I felt that some natural barriers were broken down. I do not know if the dogs felt that but I do know they did learn something also. Not all human beings are a threat. As we left the area to continue on our journey, I thought I would name the leader Duke. This seemed like a good name for one so smart and a good leader to the pack.

The Wild horses

A great part of the architecture which contributes to the landscape is the wild horses that run free. The wild mustangs are awesome and majestic. They have the stallion I called Storm lead the pack. I call him that because of his fiery attitude and his ability to change in an instant. You could see him coming but do not know what to expect. We were never in danger as long as we stayed out of his way. He was very protective of his herd and his leadership qualities were quite evident. They ran free on the other side of the fenced area we designate as our ranch.

One of my greatest moments was when Lucky Jo, Kelly and I went out on one of our adventures in the spring. It was close to the summer when Storm would bring the herd into view so we could see the colts that were born to the herd. He was a proud father to his children even though he did not sire them all. The other males did accommodate the mares but Storm seemed to take credit for it. His role was much like Grandparents to their children. We call them ours when, in reality, they belong to the parents, your children. We are just as proud and cannot wait for them to be a part of the family. Legacy has a tremendous bearing on our heritage and self-esteem. We draw off of who we are as our family accumulates in size and we all become a part of each other. We watch out for our own.

Watching this great parade of these marvelous horses, we could see one of the horses struggling to keep up. She had a colt running by her side trying to keep up with the others. We did not want to interfere but we could see the struggling mare and we wanted to help. Lucky Jo, Kelly and I began running with the herd and fortunately they were not threatened. We caught up with the mare and her colt. She was lagging behind so it was easy to separate her from the herd. She is wild but she is hurting. We had to do something and I was not sure what it would be.

First of all, we needed to stop the horse and colt to quite them. Lucky Jo played the part of helping the mare settle down, letting her know we were not a threat to her or her colt. We were able to stop her and the colt stayed close. The other horses continued on their quest for showing off the new family members. They instinctively know if you cannot keep up than you will not survive the wild. It may sound cruel but the mare was a problem to the herd. I guess it is the survival of the fittest. The colt would remain with the herd and another mare would have taken over if the mother died. Right now the colt needed to stay with its mother. He knew she needed help and did not want to separate from her.

As it was with the deer, the mare seemed to be cautious but did not feel threatened. Kelly again, took care to see the colt was okay. I approached the mare with a voice that could soothe and the horse would feel a sense of us wanting to help them and not hurt them. The mare did allow me to come closer and as I observed her I could see in her eyes she was in pain. As I brushed my hand across her back and petted her neck, I could feel her trembling inside. I knew she was sick and hurting. She being wild I could not put Lucky Jo's harness to her mouth. All I could do would be to try to get her to walk with me back to the ranch. I knew the colt would follow but to get her to follow direction, I was not sure.

I talked to her and she must have understood what I was saying, not by what words I was using but the tone I presented them with. I encouraged her to come with us as I held her head in my hand. I gently took her mane and this was the signal to go to her. We started walking back to the ranch and it was a slow journey. It was approaching dinner time and I knew my uncle was expecting me back. He knew from experience that my "Adventures" did take us quite a while, but the house rule was to be home for dinner. You did not need a watch to know that. Your tummy was the best indicator of what time it was and to head home.

My uncle was very aware that we had not returned when we were expected home. He and Robert saddled up to come looking for us. He knew what direction we headed out; in our morning discussion I did express a desire to see if I could find the wild herd of horses to see if it would be their traditional fashion show. He knew exactly where the best place to observe was so that was their first decision to look for us there. He knew that Lucky Jo and Kelly would take care of me but that did not mean that I did not need help. They felt better coming out to see if we were in trouble. They also knew Kelly would come and get them but what if Kelly was unable to. Regardless of what the circumstances were, they decided to look for us. Basically, it was concern not fear.

I do not know how long we were walking but I was getting tired and hungry. It was not so much the hunger but I knew my uncle would use that as a time frame I should be home. I did expect he would come looking for us. Actually this was my prayer, because I certainly needed his help. The mare needed attention and I knew how sick she was. She must have known herself because she did not try to run but was happy we were there. Her priority is her colt. The colt by her side, we continued toward the ranch. On horseback a mile or two is nothing. On foot, a mile or two with a sick horse is a long, intense distance. My prayers were answered when I could see my uncle and Robert approaching from the north. Their timing and sense of realizing we were on a rescue mission, they did approach with caution. I explained what happened and they were there to help.

They were able to put a rope around the mare's neck so she would follow behind. Her walk was labored and she had a difficult time holding up her head. I could mount Lucky Jo and we all headed for the ranch. It was about dusk when we reach the barn. Robert and my uncle took the mare and her colt to an area they treat and keep the sick or injured horses. It is better to quarantine them from the other horses until it is determined what the horse was sick from. Once they reached the area of confinement, the mare laid down and the colt beside her.

Even though she was wild, she knew she was in trouble. Upon examination, my uncle found that she had a temperature and was carrying some kind of infection. Often after a mare gives birth, there can be complications. Being in the wild, she could have caught something from the environment or it could have come from within. I could see that the colt had a hard time nursing. He wanted the milk but there was not much there. This could be the fact that the mare's milk was drying up because of the infection; this was protecting the colt in one sense but he was starving. It did not take much to realize that the colt was hungry and probably did not have sufficient nutrition for quite a while.

We came to the rescue of the colt and were able to feed him milk. You could see that the colt was starved. We controlled the amount all through the night because we did not want him to take too much at a time. It was better for the colt to eat small amounts more often.

We nursed the colt and we did what we could for the mother. We did separate the two, but kept them close to one another. The colt could see its mother and did sense she was taken care of. We did as little handling because of their wild nature but they were both in need of our help. The temperature of the mother would not break and she slipped into unconsciousness. Our hopes of her survival were dimishishing and we could see it would take a miracle to save her. We continued to do what we could throughout the night. I did go to bed reluctantly but as my uncle made me aware that I would need my sleep so I could continue nursing the both of them.

I did awake and my aunt made me eat breakfast. As I was trying to eat, she shared a similar story of what we were experiencing now. She gave me some worthy advice and did encourage me that the mare in that situation did survive. It will take a lot to get her through this, but that it was possible, not probable. After my breakfast, I went to the barn. The colt was quite rambunctious and nervous. The feeding was working for him; his strength was returning. He continued to keep his eye on his mother.

I cautiously approached the mare. She was still lying down and very still. I could see in her eye that she was still sick. Her nose was running and it did not look good. I asked Robert how she was through the night and he told me that her temperature did try to spike but they were able to keep it under control.

I was feeling such a sense of helplessness and such a desire to do something, I had an idea that I mentioned to my uncle. I thought maybe if I went to get Chief, the Indian, he could possibly help. I knew Princess and Ahoe had an endless knowledge of horses and possibly they could help. I saddled up Lucky Jo and went to tell them of our situation and if they thought they could help. As I arrived moving fast, they knew something was wrong. I related the situation and wanted to know if they thought they could help. Chief responded immediately, gathered some things and we were off. Princess and Ahoe also came with us. They wanted to support us and be there if they were needed. Mostly if was to be with me but they did not say that but I knew. I would have done the same thing if it were the other way around.

As we got back to the barn, they focused their eyes on the colt. He was a beauty and getting better all the time. Wild horses are a breed of their own because of their free nature. The possibility to run free all their lives was a desire of any animal. Personally I am so happy that our trained horses have allowed themselves to be domesticated because I love having a relationship with them. They all have their own purpose in this life. Thank God that my uncle gave me Lucky Jo to be my soul mate. I cannot imagine life without him.

Chief, my uncle and Robert all work diligently with the mare. It seems that they would make headway and then the fall back. It was so hard to see her go through this. The only comfort is that if she was in the wild and we had not rescued her, she would have died already. It still did not look good.

The day continued to be a repeat of the night before. Chief had brought some liquid he prepared for his horses and fed it to her a little at a time. He told me that it was like an antibiotic to humans. If they could reverse the infection, there would be hope. I was able to get in on the nursing care and administer the homemade medication. She could hardly swallow but her attempts did help. She has a strong spirit and will; that could be her best asset right now. She was literally fighting for her life. The presence of her colt gave her more courage to try.

Between caring for the mare, the colt and doing what I had to do on the ranch, my day was full. No matter how desperate the situation with the mare, I needed to focus on other things. That is typical of ranch life. No matter what the situation, you need to move from one thing to the next. The other animals needed tending too and fed, groomed and put through their regular routine. Lucky Jo, Kelly, Fudzer and I all had our daily tasks and I was a big part of theirs. It was my job to see to their needs. It was such a pleasure to do for them because of the love I have for them. This was not work. It is like taking care of your children and their needs. It is physical in one sense but the joy in doing is a real pleasure. I happen to like work. It feels good while doing and is satisfying when it is done. This is the nurturing part of our nature. I would hate living in a world where I did not do anything. Caring for the animals is as enjoyable as having fun with them. This is not work to me.

Busy taking care of my chores, my uncle approached me and told me that the mare was suffering. He needed me to go to her now because they were going to have to make a decision. Knowing what this meant, being brave was not the feelings that were in me. At this moment it was about me losing her not what was best for her. Entering the stall, she could not lift her head to look at me. Holding her head, we talked for a few minutes. They did assure me she was in no pain, at least not in the physical. With my maternal instincts, my need was to tell her we would take good care of her colt.

Stroking her head, speaking some more, preparing myself for the inevitable. Knowing this was good-bye, I did believe in the miracle that she would recover but God knew she was too ill to survive the wild. The infection was too severe, and it was affecting her brain. God answered my prayer the way it was best for her. As much as this hurt, trusting God was even more important to me.

Leaving the stall, my uncle, Robert and Chief came in to do what they had to do. They were equipped with medicine that would put her down without any pain or fear. My uncle related to me afterward that it was almost as though the mare thanked him for the relief of her situation. Also, he felt she believed me that we would care for her colt.

We let the colt come close enough to witness her death. The colt would need a sense of knowing that she was gone. We let the colt by her until he was ready to leave. We did encourage the colt to leave but did not rush it. We still had time before removing the mare's body.

My concern for the colt now is what were we going to do with him? He is wild but he could be trained. Finding a nursing mare that would adopt the colt was going to be difficult. All of our mares have weaned their colts and they did not have milk anymore.

Chief came up with a suggestion. With a little insight from Princess and Ahoe, they reminded him of their mare that just lost her colt. It was soon enough that her milk had not dried up. The only problem was would she take to this colt or not? They are both females so this could be in the best interest of the colt. We all agreed and I was happy we at least had an attempt for a solution. Chief was able to escort the colt to his place and we thought it would be better to let them go alone. We did not want the colt to get too attached to us or the place his mother died. Mother's body was removed and buried, but her scent was still in the barn. We needed to release the colt as soon as possible. There was still the question if the colt would take to the new mare or if the new mare would let this colt near her. Animal adoption is different from people adoption. We make choices and decisions. We can accept or deny. Animals decide on instinct, and this will determine the outcome.

They reached their place and we watched from a distance. Promising my uncle I would not interfere, watching from a distance to witness the bonding of the colt and mare was my intention. Lucky Jo, Kelly and I had a good view of the pasture Chief was holding the mare in so she could be separated from the other horses. It was almost a time for mourning for her until she was ready to be put back into the social situation with the other horses.

The colt was a typical child, one minute in mourning for his mom and the next wanting to play. Children have such a unique way of dealing with life. There is an inborn reality of life and death. The circle of life and death is very much a part of living. It is just that death is harder to cope with because it is loss and permanent but we all know that life will eventually lead to death.

The mare was standing quite still and could see the colt. In her observation, she watched as the colt came into the fenced corral. The colt was not used to this confinement but felt a need to approach the mare. Cautiously the colt made his way to the mare waiting for instruction from the mare. It was almost as if the colt wanted a hug as we human would response with empathy. The mare did not know that the colt was an orphan, but her motherly instincts told her not to worry. The colt came closer and put his nose to hers. Surprisingly, the mare responded with a fondling gesture.

There was a bonding of acceptance but would the mare allow the colt to nurse?

There was almost a ritual taking place as the mare and colt moved around each other. The mourning mare seemed to pick up her spirits after the loss of her foal. The emptiness seemed to be filling up with another emotion of acceptance. There must have been a communication we could not see or hear but the mare and colt were bonding. The mare must have sensed the colts need to nurse because the colt wanted to come to the mare to nurse. She was cautious but the mare was receptive. The colt was given permission by the mare to nurse and she was probably so thankful because she wasn't able to nurse from her mother very much. Her new mother had an abundance of milk but her lost foal did not have much of an opportunity before he died. Her milk was plentiful. The acceptance of each other was beautiful and it helped with the sadness of the mare's death. At least we could save her colt and save the new mother from having to live without her child.

We kept in contact with Chief on the well-being of the colt. Her ability to bounce back will depend on what kind of a horse she is going to be. Her new mother is a domestic horse so the colt will probably be broken to be used for the Indians or sold at auction for someone else. The horse ranchers do look out for one another, as well as the Indians on the reservation. Chief would make the right decision for the colt. There are no guarantees for the colt but right now her changes are excellent.

CHAPTER 5: The Trip

Off to the Fair

There was an opportunity for me to show off Lucky Jo in the annual fair that was in a nearby town. We look forward to this every year and my pride excels as Lucky Jo just shines. He qualifies so well in each category. This being a western riding area, we have a lot of western style challenges to overcome. It is in a rodeo fashion and we have more fun running the races, barrel runs which take you around barrels in a pattern, and showing off the skills of your horse. Lucky Jo is phenomenal when it comes to being capable. He can do so many things and is so smart. I think he is half human but that would not be as much fun. He takes direction and commands so well. It is as if he can read my mind.

I know Lucky Jo looks forward to this so he can show off his talents and be praised for them. My praise is enough but a little stroking from others certainly can boost your ego. Even horses need that assurance that they are special. Children are no different.

Preparing the trailer to take Lucky Jo to the fair, my uncle and Robert make sure everything is done right. Lucky Jo is a great traveler and believe this or not, Fudzer rides on Lucky Jo's back for the trip. Kelly rides in the front of the truck with me; she keeps watch for what is ahead. She is the one looking out for us. Lucky Jo and Fudzer have blind vision so they do not get spooked on the trip. It is much like putting blinders on his eyes. Fudzer was fine in the trusting hands of Lucky Jo, as you might say. She was happy to be going along.

Everything secure and tied down, my uncle said they would be following behind in a little while. They needed to get some work done at the ranch and then I could get Lucky Jo settled down for the competition. They would meet us there in time for the races to begin.

Looking forward to this, being with my best friends, and showing off Lucky Jo is such a joy. His reputation preceded him and if you were a gambling person, he was the favorite. His sense of timing and his ability to respond so quickly to the situation made him stand out among the others. We knew there would be new competition because over the winter you have no idea what the new horses were capable of in their training. This thought of new competition was just another opportunity for Lucky Jo to "Strut his Stuff".

The trip was going to take about an hour. Packing a few staples, we were traveling light. We had water, some sandwiches thanks to my aunt, and music that was appealing for the trip. Being a pretty traditional person, when it comes to things like that, it makes me comfortable. I like music that makes sense, puts you in a positive mood, and soothing to the ears. Kelly also agreed with my choice of the listening sound. Admiring the day with its beauty even though there were clouds overhead, the weather prediction was some rain. Where our destination was, it was to be clear skies. It is amazing to me that you can be in one place and the weather would be one thing; travel up the ride a ways and it can change. This is why I love to travel, the changing scenery, temperature and view. It is all the same beautiful country but with different moods and attitudes. Of course the temperature, wind, sun, moisture all play a role in these changing styles, but that is what makes "America the Beautiful"

The weather started changing quite abruptly. Surprised by the rain that came down so suddenly, it seemed that one minute a few clouds and overcast, then the sky opened up and dumped water down on us. Immediately rolling up my window, the sudden change of temperature caused the windows to cloud up and it was hard to see. An uncomfortable feeling came over me knowing Lucky Jo and Fudzer were in the trailer. I was pulling the trailer and Kelly is the truck with me. Responsible for their well-being, I took this very serious. Besides that, my love for them is a dying love; just as you feel for your child. These were my children and best friends while staying with my uncle

I tried wiping the window of clouding but it seemed to return as quickly as before. Slowing down was an option but not being able to see ahead was frightening. In fact with the hard rain and the moisture that covered the window, I could not see to pull off to a safe area until the rained stopped. We could wait it out but the area is too unfamiliar. This is my greatest concern but I had to seek safety for all of us and this is the mission at hand.

The Accident

The rain continued and my struggle to find a place seemed almost impossible but having faith to believe we could find the right spot. Continually to pray for the Lord's guidance to help us find that spot did give me comfort. All of the sudden there was such an impact, I could feel my seat belt tighten, the shatter of glass and the truck is out of control. The sound was horrible with breaking metal, a screech of brakes, and then feeling nothing. Going into an unconscious state, this deep sleep lasted for about three days. Regaining consciousness, there was an awareness of some terrible pain in my body. My head was throbbing with unbearable pain. There was something wrapped around my head. My face hurt telling me it was swollen. There was vision out of only one eye. There was pain in my abdomen and my leg was hurting. Afraid to move, there was no question looking around where I was. It was a hospital with all the trimmings; machines, monitors, wires, tubes and sounds. Looking at the machines, there were all sorts of lines and numbers recording. At least as long as the numbers and noises continued I was alive. This was not heaven recognizing the hospital atmosphere and the last thing I remember is taking a tumble in the truck, feeling pain and then nothing. All went black.

Regaining consciousness, my aunt was there with her beautiful face and smile. It was a wonderful feeling knowing she was there; she could tell me what was wrong and what had happened. She hugged me gently because she knew I was hurting but I did not care, it was worth it.

As she began to relate what had happened, she assured me that everyone was alright. It was a terrible accident and unfortunately we never made it to the fair. It seems that in my desperation to find a place to pull over, an oncoming truck side swiped us because he could not see and the torrential rain was clouding his vision. He was also trying to find an escape route to put his truck to rest when his brakes gave way, he lost control of the truck. This collision caused us to take a tumble down a ravine. The truck and trailer simultaneously went into a roll and did stay together. They rolled as one unit, helping Lucky Jo and Fudzer maintain them in the trailer. Lucky Jo did not roll over on Fudzer. She was able to follow Lucky Jo around. He was in a panic mode but when the trailer stopped, Lucky Jo laid still and unresponsive. Fudzer was scared but stayed to comfort Lucky Jo.

Kelly and I entwined with each other. Fortunately I had on my seat belt and we had fashioned a type of seat belt for Kelly. She was restrained to keep her with the truck and safe. When the truck stopped its roll, Kelly knew I was hurt. She whimpered and tried to reach me. There was not enough distance in the front seat so she could not reach me. She had to tend to her own wounds. Apparently, she was cut by broken glass as it shattered while in our freefall roll. Her wounds were superficial but none-the-less painful. She also was trapped between me and the crumple metal. Her door had given in when the truck and trailer came to rest. Water was coming in open areas, making things even worse.

My uncle and Robert, who were following behind us about ten minutes away, came upon the scene. Their vision is impaired also with the rain so it took awhile before they realized that the accident up ahead was us. Their heart sank as they got closer. By the time they reached us, there were other people who witnessed the accident; they stopped to see if they could do anything. Apparently the driver of the truck was also unconscious and trapped in his truck. We do have a means of communication in the area; there isn't much help in-between towns. Truckers have their CB radios and we were equipped with an emergency radio. They could not get to ours but one of the witnesses who came to assist was able to call for help.

Help Arrives

The first rescue person on the scene was trying to assess the situation and what was the priority. The trailer latch in the back opened and he could see Lucky Jo and Fudzer. Lucky Jo still was not moving. He went to my truck and could see me not moving but breathing. The blood was visible and he knew I was in a serious condition. He could not move me because he was afraid of complicating my injuries. He was going to leave that to the professionals.

He was able to get to Kelly and release her. Kelly understood he was there to help and was thankful he was.

She was so concerned about me. After he did release her, she immediately came to me and saw no movement. She licked my wounds and tried to awaken me. She was not successful and she did let the stranger try to see what was wrong with her. He could see the wounds but did feel that they were not too serious. Kelly went back to the trailer and with the back opened she was able to go inside. She saw Fudzer, gave her a welcome lick but realized Lucky Jo was not moving either. She licked him but no response. She came to me to tell me about Lucky Jo but still no response either.

By this time, my uncle and Robert arrived, the stranger knew they were family; they all pitched in to see what they could do. My uncle must have worked on me with pure adrenaline. He did not give himself the option of feeling the emotional pain because that would interfere with his judgment. He needed to focus on the situation at hand.

The rescue sirens were fast approaching. In the emergency call a Veterinary was called for assistance because Lucky Jo was involved, with Kelly and Fudzer. He came with a transport for the horse. It was capable of loading Lucky Jo onto it without causing more injury. An ambulance arrived as well as a rescue vehicle. Their job was to get the driver of the truck and myself out of our trapped position. This is so difficult with such complicated injuries. They needed to free us without causing more injury.

The Vet came with tools and torches so they could cut away the side of the horse trailer, then they could lift Lucky Jo out of the trailer. He was still unconscious but alive. They were busy doing what they came to do and their concern was for the animals. Fudzer stayed with Lucky Jo and they did transport Kelly with him also. It was best to keep them together and then the Vet could examine them all. It took time to cut away the side of the trailer and the interference of the rain continued to be an obstruction. They had no choice but to tolerate it and try to ignore its presence. Finally Lucky Jo was being lifted on the transport and the design was quite unique. The bed was flat with removable sides and top. This way Lucky Jo could be laid on the flat bed and then the sides and top put into place. Kelly and Fudzer were able to ride with him as they went to the Vet's hospital for care.

In the meantime, the rescue crew came to assist me and the driver of the truck. They worked simultaneously on both of us. They could not determine who was the more injured but being that we were both unconscious, they were not going to chose. They worked as hard and as fast as they could to free us both. As far as they could tell, they needed the Jaws of Life to free me from the truck. I was pinned in a position that was awkward to get to. They did not want me to move, just the crumbled metal holding me intact. As they worked on my truck, they also worked on the other one. Apparently, the other truck came down the ravine and followed after us. His truck landed on all four tires, so this upright position was easier to get him out. After securing his neck with a brace, they forced the door open and removed his body. The extent of his wounds were fatal; he died at the scene of the accident.

With sparks flying, the side of my truck was giving way to the expert hands of the rescuers. Pulling, tearing, and breaking were all a part of the task to get me free. They finally were able to get to me and put a collar on me to protect my neck. After they got my body out, they secured me to a flat board so I could not move from there. They did not want to add to my already battered body. My uncle and Robert followed the rescuers up the ravine and intended to follow behind the ambulance. They had also had a chance to see that Lucky Jo, Kelly, and Fudzer were ready to be transported. As much as they loved them, I was the priority.

The Damage

As my aunt is telling me the story of the accident, wrapping my mind around the three days missed and the seriousness of the accident was difficult. My need at the moment is to know the damages that occurred and how everyone was. Feeling terrible about the driver of the other truck, what about Lucky Jo, Kelly and Fudzer? My thoughts were about them more than myself. My family came first.

She started with Lucky Jo. Once they arrived at the hospital, they used the same transporting harness to lift him off the flat bed. They removed the top and sides, just as they had done before loading him to be transported to the hospital. He was still unconscious so they had to make an evaluation of his injuries to see what extent they were. They lowered his lifeless body onto the ground where they could begin the assessment.

They had a marvelous machine that was a Cat-Scan for the animals. It would scan the entire body so the Vet could see his internal injuries. They were relieved that he did not sustain any broken bones. They determined that the unconsciousness was due to a concussion but there was no fracture. The concussion was caused by the impact and it was a good thing so his skull could rest from the trauma protecting his brain. We would not know if there was any brain damage until some of the swelling goes down. The Vet could not say for sure but they were hopeful that he would be alright.

The scan did reveal that his spleen had been damaged. It was not a difficult injury but it would call for surgery. Also, they were concerned that he may have sustained a fractured rib, hopefully not broken. This could put his lung in jeopardy. They would know more after the surgery.

The surgery was a success but we would not know how he was for a couple of days. If he did not recover from unconsciousness, they would be more concerned. For the time being, they would care for him and tend to his wounds. My uncle and Robert were so relieved that the prognosis is favorable. It was hard enough on them with me in the condition I was, let alone Lucky Jo. They could not imagine loosing both of us. Our history together is their life and we have all shared in that for years.

When they did get to the Vet after the accident, someone had already started to examine Kelly and Fudzer. Upon examination of Kelly, she suffered some cuts and needed glass removed from them. She was cooperative but shaken with the accident. Her trauma was able to be subdued by giving her drugs to help with any pain, mend her wounds and settle her down so she could sleep and get some rest. They were able to put her with Lucky Jo but not too close. If Lucky Jo should regain consciousness and decide to roll, Kelly could be a victim.

Fudzer was very quiet which was suspicious for her. Usually she is pretty frisky but her response was out of the ordinary. The Vet examined her also and found that she was okay but in what he called a State of Trauma. She was not unconscious but what she had been through was described to us like she is awake but asleep. She would probably be alright but she needed to be watched closely; she may stay in this state of trauma and never come out of it. Her mind and body could not take what she had experienced. It may have been too much for her. She was on a twenty-four hour watch and they ministered some medicine so she would stay calm and rest her mind and body. This was the best care for her right now.

Now that she told me about my family, I needed to know about me. She told me about the concussion with a fracture. They did surgery to release blood that was bleeding in the brain. They put a shunt in my head so the bleeding would have passage out of the brain. The swelling was a problem because there could be brain damage but they felt at this point, it would take care of itself. They would watch me closely.

My swollen eye was not injury to my eye. It was the impact of something my eye came in contact with. The vision in that eye is alright, but we have to wait for the swelling to come down. I suffered a large cut on my head which resulted in the blood that covered my face. This is the area of the fractured skull. They put a large number of stitches in so that the scar would eventually be unnoticeable.

The pain in my stomach area was a major bruising I received from the roll or the impact. It was sore but not serious. My leg was broken and another surgery took care of the damage. The directions were to stay off my leg about three months until the screws they implanted to hold the bone in my leg fused together. Fortunately it was not the ankle which does take longer to heal and is more difficult to recover from.

My days in the hospital were numbered as my healing progressed. My head injury was healing well, my stomach was getting better and my leg was feeling less pain. If my recovery continued to do this well, they could let me go home to recover. The instructions were that I needed to be eating normal, drinking fluids, and off any medication from the IV. Mostly it was for pain and an antibiotic to prevent infection. My feeding came from a feeding tube in my stomach because my throat swelled up from the accident. The tube had to stay in as long as I could not eat. It would stay in my stomach until I could eat everything normally. With the help of my aunt, the feeding could be continued at home. It was not difficult to do, just a bit anxious for those who would have to do it.

After about three weeks in the hospital, they did another Cat-Scan on my head and leg to determine how the healing was coming along. If they felt my head was doing well, they would consider letting me get up out of bed. They did not want the brain to start bleeding or swelling again. The shunt used to release built up blood was working well. They changed my bandages often.

The Cat-Scan was very positive. They could see the brain was back to normal, the fracture was healing and there was no more danger. My leg revealed that the screws they implanted to hold my broken bone together was fusing to the bone on both sides of the break. They also put "cages is what they called them" to help with the fusion. They needed to put ground bone in these cages to help the broken area. It was a pretty bad break so they needed to give help to the injury. The bone came from a piece of my hip so they could fuse the bone together. This bone was in the cages. Actually it was quite fascinating what they did if you can think beyond the injury.

They were able to observe my abdomen where the bruised area was and it was healing nicely. They were also able to observe the feeding tube and determined it was correctly in place. After the doctor got the results of the Cat-Scan he could give us a timeline of about three more weeks if all continued going as well as it was. The three weeks passed, another Cat-San and the results were amazing. I was given permission to go home.

Lucky Jo regained consciousness about two days after the accident. His surgery was also successful, it would just take time. He needed help to get to his feet and he needed to get up. They were afraid that if he stayed down his lungs would fill with fluid and he could get pneumonia. If he did not regain consciousness, there is nothing we could do. We could not put him up in a harness because of his injuries and the surgery. We would have been helpless and possibly had to watch him die. I praise the Lord we did not have to bare this burden. He got up on his own. They knew he wondered about me so they put a picture of me up in his stall with the bandages on and possibly he would understand. At least he could see me.

Kelly did have a broken leg and needed several stitches for her wounds. The greater challenge was removing the glass that penetrated her skin at the time of the accident. They did put a splint on her leg and she walked on her three legs. She managed beautifully. Her concern was Me, Lucky Jo and Fudzer. Kelly could also see my picture and I believe in my heart she understood. She stayed close to Lucky Jo. In fact she stayed by his side all the time he was unconscious.

Fudzer did not have any injuries that were visible. Her injury was from the trauma she sustained. As the vet told us, she may or may not recover. She stayed close to Lucky Jo also. She spent most of her time sleeping. The Vet told us that this was the best medicine for her. They gave her something to rest her brain and her thinking. It would calm her and keep her from thinking about the accident. They were hopeful that when she found we were alright her healing would progress. Knowing she missed me so that did not help. I was gone the six weeks so the three of them had to take care of each other.

My uncle and Robert would talk about me to my family. It seemed to help because their demeanor would change when they would hear my name mentioned. Lucky Jo was able to walk around, Kelly would tag along on her three legs and a hobble, and Fudzer continued to sleep and stay silent. They knew this was good for her. Possibly when I do get home, she may come around. It will have been six weeks since the accident.

Going Home

The day has finally come for me to come home. They removed my bandages; secured my leg and the final Cat-Scan showed everything was fine, except my leg. My leg would take another couple months, and then probably a walking cast. This would be determined by how well the fusion on my leg was doing. At least the crutches will help me get up and around.

The swelling of my throat was so much better so eating normally was possible. They were able to remove the feeding tube before leaving the hospital. My aunt was so thankful for that. A visiting nurse would come three times a week to monitor my vitals and see how being home was going. Fortunately my aunt could set me up on the first floor which was a spare bedroom with a bath. When they built the house they perceived just such a situation where someone would need nursing care. There wisdom certainly was a blessing to me.

At the time of the accident my parents were notified and they came as quickly as possible. They stayed until they knew I was out of danger and would be alright. There visits in the hospital were enjoyable. My uncle's ranch was the best place to recover rather than my parents home. Besides taking care of my Lucky Jo, Kelly and Fudzer were going to be healing for me. There were constant up dates on their condition. The information was volunteered so asking was not necessary. They knew this was the best medicine for me.

My uncle's insurance company replaced the truck and trailer; a settlement from the other truck driver's insurance company made it possible to recover the loss from the accident. He did find out about the other driver and paid condolences to his family. It was so sad and unfortunate that he died. Fortunately he had insurance so his family would be taken care of, at least monetarily. This made his death a little less painful.

My uncle did invite the three children and their mother to the ranch to ride and participate in the things of the ranch. Meeting them when my hospital stay was over, was a pleasure but sad. Ironically, they became close to us and our family. We were able to contribute to their healing. We could not replace their dad but they could forget about it for a while as they got involved with the horses and riding. One of the rules of the ranch is that if you ride you have to muck the stalls (clean up the animal elimination) and anything else to be done. This responsibility and the joy of riding was teaching them so much more than just riding. The horses needed to be brushed, cleaned up after the ride, and the saddle and bridle removed. In fact, they had to saddle and bridle the horses before the ride.

The time they spent at the ranch would stay in there memory for a lifetime and thanks to my uncle and Robert, they found a new father figure. This made their mother so proud and a comfort that her children, two boys and a girl could experience this. They continued to become part of the family. In fact, they are to this day.

I had been waiting for my home coming for such a long time. My life has changed so drastically but I have faith to believe that God has something wonderful waiting for me. Trusting Him every step of the way is so necessary because there are still many uncertainties.? Thinking about where the accident had taken me and what God has brought us through this far is faith and hope. God spared our lives so there must be more He wants of us here on earth. Possibly to prove to those around me that God does give miracles today. I am living proof of that.

While riding in the truck, anxiety was causing many emotions. Confined for six weeks, the remnants of the accident began to become vivid. Feelings of stress came over me as the cars and trucks would pass us by. My uncle could see my body becoming rigid and expressing my feelings as my hands clutch my coat. He could even see my white knuckles. He made the decision to pull off the road to safety helping me to get a handle on the experience.

We stopped and we got out of the truck. He helped me because my leg was a hindrance. Up ahead we could see a ranch with horses. In the distance I could see the horses running and enjoying their existence. Watching them made me think about Lucky Jo and my uncle. This gave me a chance to talk about my feelings. The thought of losing them was unbearable. My nurturing spirit was coming out. My desire is that everything would go back to normal but the question still remains, "We do not know". The time we were spending there was probably the best therapy because by the time we reach the ranch my emotional release would be behind me. Preparing myself to greet the family after all that has happened was uncertain. My uncle was patient and was willing to wait for as long as it took.

He wanted to know if the back roads home instead of the highway would be better. It may take longer but handling the ride probably will help me adjust it better.

Thanking him for his perception, the back roads were a better choice. Relaxing was much easier in the truck. Looking ahead up the road to the ranch and now I am now getting excited. My uncle could see the relief on my face and the anticipation in my reaction. This made him feel better and he knew when I saw my loved ones, all would be okay.

As we drove into the ranch area, Kelly came running to the truck. We stopped, I opened the door and she could not lick me enough. She was all over me when she jumped into the truck. This was wonderful to see her and see her jump around. She had her cast off and was walking normal. Feeling much better from the accident and her recovery, she looked and acted fine.

Getting out of the truck she could see the bandaged leg and my crutches. She soon realized that my walking was not as fast as usual. She was patient because she wanted me to go to Lucky Jo in the barn. In the meantime, my aunt came out with her wonderful greeting; she wanted to be there when I am reunited with Lucky Jo and Fudzer. Fudzer was progressing slowly and we still do not know what her prognosis is going to be. They were hoping when I got home from the hospital things would change. We would have to wait and see.

Making my way to the barn, Lucky Jo heard my voice. Immediately he came to me with the biggest whinny, bouncing his head up and down and had to rub me with his nose. He put his face to mine rubbing it affectionately. He even did his dance around me. Dropping my crutches, I was able to hug him as never before. My heart leaped for joy not only because he was back to normal but we were united together again. My prayer is that we never have to be separated again from some unfortunate circumstance.

My uncle gave me my crutches back and we went to find Fudzer. She spends most of her time in Lucky Jo's stall. She hasn't even been catching mice which she loves to do. My uncle and the horses love that too. She is withdrawn in this state of trauma and does not want to come out. Our prayer is that now we are all together as a family, she will recover.

Approaching the stall, looking inside and she is curled up in a ball. Waiting to see if she recognizes me, gently seeking a stool to sit on, the crutches are awkward but my uncle could lift her up to me. While on the stool with a little help from my uncle, I sat down. He was able to reach Fudzer under the stool. He picked her up and handed her to me. She did not do much until I started talking to her and rubbing her. Letting her lay in my lap, we continued the bonding. She lifted her head to look at me. She looked into my eyes and she began to respond. She stood up in my lap, turned around and climbed up my chest. Holding her under her front legs, we could be face to face.

Focusing on her eyes, something was beginning to happen. It was as if a cloud was covering her eyes and it began to peel away. Not knowing if this is actually what is happening, it was what could be categorize as a miracle. Once this covering seemed to disappear, her eyes changed. I could even see my own reflection in her eyes. She meowed and wanted to lick my face. Talking to her, she continued to lick me. She looked at Lucky Jo, Kelly, my uncle and Robert. She turned back to me and began purring. She walked around my lap and then continued to climb up my chest and rub her face against mine. Bringing her up to me again, were could see each other eye to eye. Her eyes have definitely changed.

Content to be on my lap, Lucky Jo and Kelly had to welcome her back. Kelly licked her and Lucky Jo did his nose rub on her to let her know how much he wanted her to respond to him. I want to believe he knew to leave her alone and she would come around. He remained faithful believing in her recovery.

Holding Fudzer so she could look at her surroundings, this helped her to realize where she was. It was as if she needed time to re-evaluate her existence and the home she lives in. Her mind was coming back to life; I could feel a sense of shaking in her body. Actually, she has missed six weeks of her life. She did eat but it was a robot mimic. She ate, drank and then would go back to sleep. Her physical body was alright but mentally she was distraught. Her withdrawal was to protect her mind until she could get over the trauma.

We called the Vet to come out to examine her and he had never seen something this remarkable. Upon examination, he looked into her eyes and could see what I saw that she felt safe. Whether it was God or her body, I chose to believe it was God.

CHAPTER 6: The Boys and Girls Club

Learn to Work Together

Now that my family and I are reunited, we all take our assigned positions to the activity of the ranch. Fudzer was back catching mice, which made all the horses happy, especially Lucky Jo. Kelly was herself, herding in the horses, keeping watch over everything and partnering with my uncle and Robert doing the chores necessary for the ranch to function. Lucky Jo was able to run and show off his attributes which he loved doing. He was a horse that could be free around the ranch. It was almost as if he were a watch dog. This is the role he assumed and loved it. He was the king and master of his domain. At least he thought so and we let him. He is a permanent fixture around the ranch.

My recovery took a lot longer; my leg needed more time to heal. Stressing it in any way meant being careful with what I did or did not do. Helping my uncle run the ranch was enough and now a wonderful caretaker for me. She managed so well and was right there when my need did arrive. Bathing and dressing were the predominant difficulties which would last until my cast was off. They were able to put a walking cast on after three months. This certainly helped with my ability to maneuver on the ranch. I could not ride but spending time with my family was wonderful.

My cast is off, and I am back to normal, thank you Jesus. With the last Cat-Scan it showed that my head and leg were healed. The fusion on my leg was healing fine which meant living life normal aware of the fragility of my leg. Another trauma to it and they may not be able to repair my leg. In fact, a bit nervous about what did happen and could have happen is still very vivid in my mind. We are all safe and that is what is important.

One of the events that have become a ritual is that a neighboring boys and girls club is invited to the ranch to help the children in so many ways. The object is to develop a love and respect for the horses. They would learn about the ranch and what it takes to make it function as a unit. The responsibility alone is an education in itself.

It was a succession of Saturdays that the club would come and each Saturday would be a different lesson learned. After the lesson they were able to ride. This was the reward and Robert enjoyed taking them out with the horses riding.

One project is to teach them how to fence the property. This is a number one priority because your livestock has to be safe and contained. To a ranch your livestock is your bread and butter; ours is horses and most of the ranches in the area did raise horses. All of the ranches did have cows for milk and meat to carry them for the winter. We did have chickens for the eggs and food. They were there for a purpose to feed the family and the ranch hands. Our business was breeding and raising horses. These were the "special horses" that we claim as ours. Lucky Jo was my horse and no one else rode him. When I was away they took care of him just as if he were theirs.

The boys and girls did learn to work together. They found that work first then fun. A ranch needs to have its needs met early in the morning. When the rooster crows, the wake up call has been initiated. Everyone is expected to rise and shine, whether they feel like it or not. Being tired from the day before is no excuse. They would come on Friday evening so they could experience the morning routine. We had extra bunk beds in the bunk house just for these kids. It was clean and comfortable and Robert kept it in good shape because this is where he choose to live. He was invited to the table to eat with all of us; he is family. The bunk house did have a bathroom and a shower which were all the comforts of home

The rooster crowed, the sun was rising and the work begins. You were to work about an hour before breakfast. This week it was gathering the eggs for the hen house, and bringing them to my aunt so she could cook the eggs for breakfast. This is done everyday but today it was the visiting club to do the job. They were given instructions how to retrieve the eggs and watch out for the rooster. He is protective of his brood so you have to respect his space.

When you enter the hen house you have to be patient and move cautiously so you are not a threat. In a calm reassuring voice tell the chicken what you are there for and not to worry. The kids were strangers so the chickens were not used to their presence. They took turns going in and out of the hen house. We did inform them that if one did decide to attack, just be still. Do not retaliate as you would normally do because you are in their hen house; you are the intruder.

The rooster and the chickens did cooperate and the kids were successful this time. We were glad because we did not want to frighten them but we needed to prepare them for the worse. They gathered the eggs and my uncle showed them how some of the eggs are fertilized and they will be incubated for new chickens. The life cycle is a part of the necessity of the ranch. Some are eggs, some are for laying hens and some are for food. It is quite a job to keep the chicken life cycle to continue so every step is important and necessary. Teaching the kids this was quite fascinating to them.

We took the gathered eggs to my aunt so she could cook them for breakfast. She made her own bread and we had bacon and ham from the pig we had slaughter.

We did not want to raise pigs so my uncle made a deal with the pig farmer to give them a colt for a slaughtered pig. We would freeze it and use all the meat until we needed another one. Between the cows and the pig we had all the meat necessary to sustain us for six months to a year; this would depend upon how many we needed to feed. The needs of the ranch depended upon how many we had to feed. There were times we had to call in extra help especially when the crops came in. When the mares were delivering their foals is another example. It seems that some things just all happened at the same time.

We were able to borrow a neighboring bull for the purpose of impregnating the cows when they were in heat. All you had to do was turn the bull loose out in the pasture with the cows and let nature takes its course. I cannot explain how the bull new he was done but when he had finished his duty, he would come close to the fence and we knew it was time to go home. Personally I felt he thought he had the best job of all. This did not matter because he was there to help us. The cycle of the cows and calving can continue.

Before breakfast it was milking the cows. They needed milking two to three times a day, depending on the cow. We did have milking machines in the dairy barn so it was not the back breaking job it used to be. All you had to do was fasten the coupler to the utter and the machine did the work. The cows were not afraid of the sound and were relieved to be milked. Any nursing mother knows how painful it is when your breast fills with milk and it is time to nurse your baby. You are so relieved to have the pressure of full breast released. The cows are the same way. In fact, the more you milk the more milk is produced.

We would transport the milk we did not need to a neighboring dairy farm and they would exchange it with other milk products. We would have pasteurized milk, cheese, and butter all in return. It was more cost effective to use this barter system to get what each other needed for our health. This is what I loved so much about ranch life. It was the working together to help one another achieve the same goal. This translates into every aspect of our life.

Taking Care of the Horses

Not everyone has a passion for horses like I do but they can learn to love and respect them. They are such a wonderful, powerful animal; they have the ability to make you feel quite insignificant. Learning to control them will help you control yourself. If you let your guard down you can be the victim and the horse is the victor.

Everyone needs something greater than themselves to show you that you are not an entity only to you. We have got to learn how to give and take thinking of others first. Self satisfaction is a no win situation. You can never get enough and reach your full potential. God is the only thing that will fill you up. The minute you stop growing and stop learning will be a sad day in your life. When growth stops then you are not significant to the world around you. There is always something you can do for someone else.

The training with the horses begins not with the riding but the taking care of and becoming familiar with them. You need to feel comfortable around them so when you do mount one, you will have already connected with them. It is learning to understand their wants and needs and to be a part of their care taking. There is the feeding, watering, grooming, and mucking the stalls. If you do not want to clean the stall, you do not care about the horse. You need to think of the caring and cleaning of the horse and meeting his needs. Regardless of how you feel about it, it is necessary. Think in your own mind how you would feel. Horses are no different. Giving them the attention is connecting with them to where they recognize you and you are not a threat to them.

Picking out any pet to be yours is not an easy thing to do. If you were looking for a dog or cat, you may feel they are all cute but in your heart you are looking for a connection or potential bond between the two of you. Your parents will give the practical side to the choice but the decision is yours. You look at all the choices of the pets to be taken but then you spot the pet that is "the one" you were destined to be with. You have already felt the "something special" that gives you the ability to choose one among many. You cannot express exactly why this is the right choice, you just know in your heart.

As the boys and girls come to the ranch, they are able to choose the horse they want to adopt as their own. Eventually it is possible for them to have the horse depending upon the parent's perspective; it will be theirs. This decision is also dependent upon how they measure up as care takers of the horse. This is where we will decide if they can have the horse.

One of the girls came with a desire to learn all she could about the ranch. She always wanted a horse but her parents were never in one place long enough. Now they had settled in the area and had obtain some land they were going to try to ranch. Their background was with horses and ranching but had strayed from their childhood up bringing. Her parents met in college, married just after graduation, pursued their careers and now they were ready to come back to their roots. The girl loved hearing the stories her parents would tell about the place they grew up with horses.

One of our horses was a painted one, brown and white, a gift from Chief and his family. She was a two year old and ready to be trained. She was not as large as the average horse but to this girl, Mary, she was perfect. She found the spiritual connection with the horse that I have described. As Mary approached the horse, she was cautious but confident. I was there to help the horse with the introduction. All we were interested in at the moment was a sense of feel and if the two could respond to each other. As we talked to the horse we would run our hands over her and look her in the eye. This is where trust begins. You have to feel comfortable and talk to the horse eye to eye, non-threatening but with assurance. The horse will know if you are afraid. If you are afraid than you have already lost the battle.

We started walking with Paint, the name we gave the horse, in the corral. If Paint decided she did not like us, it gave us a sense of security because she could be contained. The horse began to relax as I could feel her taunt muscles straining. Mary did a good job of talking to Paint and giving her reassurance. We were definitely making headway. Part of Mary's training will be eventually teaching the horse to depend on her but still self sufficient. We certainly do not want our horses to be robots.

By becoming familiar with the routine of the horses it kept them busy. There was no time for riding at this point. Work first and then play. In the beginning, it is all work because they have to learn the order of running a ranch. If my uncle did not manage his time and priorities, nothing would be accomplished.

Lucky Jo and Kelly really enjoyed the time the children were there. Kelly would play tag with the kids but we know who won that one with Kelly being a herding dog. The "Throw the Stick" game was much fairer because the kids did not have to compete.

The children learned to undo the bails of hay in the barn so the livestock could eat. They learned to put the livestock out in the pasture to graze. Naturally with the children I came into the barn and I saw a train of children jumping from the loft into cut opened bails of hay. I thought they had a great idea. Playing "King of the Castle" and your opponent goes off the loft into the hay below. There was the occasional "Geronimo" as they go flying off the platform. Me the adult in charge and I did the appropriate thing and joined them.

There is nothing greater in the world of laughing children having good old fashioned fun. My Aunt Millie and Uncle Nick got such a kick out of me. They looked forward to the beginning of the summer when school was out and dreaded the end of summer when I had to go back. This was the life cycle at this time in my life. I was so thankful for the opportunity trying not to focus on the negative. Always happy and cheerful with my Aunt and Uncle, they did not want to face the fact that eventually it was time to leave.

Riding Lessons

We have come to the place where it is time for the boys and girls to learn to ride. They have been taking care of the horse they chose; now the reward in learning how to ride. Getting on the back right now is steps away.

First they have to bridle the horse. This means to put the metal of the bridle in his mouth, have him accept it and then pull the bridle over his head. We had to help with this because some of the kids could not reach over the horses head. This is where "the box" comes in. Just as you would stoop down to talk to a child, you need to be up to face the eyes of the horse. He needs to know you are doing this and decides if he wants you to do it. Forcing any animal to do anything he does not want to is a formula for disaster. If the horse decides this is not the time, you will honor that and try another time.

Your horse agrees that you can bridle him, and then you walk around the corral with the horse. You try to lead the horse to begin the process of getting in control with respect; if he decides he wants to be first, you give him the right of way. This is no time to battle.

As you make the journey around the corral, you have a good time talking to your horse. Tell him how you are feeling and the relationship that is developing into intimacy. This is a perfect time for the kids to tell the horse how they are feeling about themselves and their lives. Your horse does care how you feel. It is not the words; it is the confidence you are sharing with the horse. Somehow your horse understands you will not betray your trust. The horse cannot speak and the person feels so much better for having a friend to talk to.

Once you feel the connection with your horse and you feel confident with moving forward to saddling your horse, the process begins. First, it is the blanket, then the saddle and then to secure the saddle with the cinch. It drops down on the far side so you can pull it under the belly of the horse. The cinch is what holds you and the saddle with the horse.

You do not mount the horse yet because you want your horse comfortable with the saddle. If he does not like the saddle, he is not going to like you on his back. Give him the opportunity to tell you if he is ready or not. If not, then you wait until another time. In the meantime, you walk with him bridled and having your intimate conversations.

Assuming your horse is ready to be saddled, you get "the box" and place it at the left side of the horse. You walk in front of him getting it so he can see you and know it is not a threatening jester. You tell him what you are going to do with confidence and let him know that you want to do this. Your actions need to be firm to show your confidence but your voice will show the love.

As you step up onto the box the blanket is first, this is fine. You will need help with throwing the saddle over the back of the horse. The horse is familiar with us so this is comfortable for him. Whether he handles the saddle on his back is another situation. You are standing on the box to grab the saddle as it comes flying over. The cinch stays on the right side ready to attach the saddle to the horse on the left side. You give the horse a chance to feel the saddle and you reach under the horse to get the cinch.

You need to tell your horse what you are going to do before you do it. You look into his eye and tell him. He will be focusing on you, not the saddle. When you feel that the horse agrees, you reach under holding your other hand on the horse. You do not want to break the connection you have established with the horse. As you retrieve the cinch, bring it under the horse and then fasten it on the left side. The horse seems to feel comfortable so you can feel accomplished with this part of the task.

Now it is time to mount the horse. Before actually mounting the real horse, we have a set-up that we have a saddle mounted to a block of wood so the new learners can put their foot in the stirrup; they throw their leg over while pulling them up. Once they feel they can handle this comfortably and confident, that they are ready to mount a real horse. They will be able to focus on the horse, be in control and not worry about being able to get up on the horse. You have eliminated a step to help the person mounting for the first time.

The mounting begins with getting "the box", talking to your horses and having help with this process. When you feel your horse is ready, you attempt your first mount. A horse is usually 15 to 17 hands high. This measurement is putting your hands sideways, one on top of the other, from the ground up to the top of the horse. It is an approximate number but accurate to describing the height of the horse.

You need to feel a sense of assurance for you and the horse. When you mounted the horse you had the bridle straps in your hand. When mounting the horse you have the bridle straps in your hand. You need to be able to control the horse if he decides he does not want you up there. You do have a handle or knob on the western saddle so you can grab this to hold on. We prefer that you do not want to use it unless you have to. It is there to use, so use it if necessary. Do not let go of the reins because this is your steering wheel, as it would be for a car.

You stay in this position until you feel you are ready to proceed. You need to feel that if the horse does not want you up there and take your direction, he will try to buck you off his back. This is the worse possible scenario, but you need this knowledge in order to expect it and be prepared. If you have done all the preliminaries, this is very unlikely.

Your knees will be what you will squeeze if you feel like you are going to fall or to hold on in a turn. You will learn that your body will automatically respond to any situation but for now, this is one of the tools to use to help you. At first, you will have someone walk with the horse while you are saddled up and getting that wonderful feeling of riding a horse. If you are afraid the horse will sense it. If you do think you are going to be afraid, then do not mount. Wait until you are ready.

Acting confident, sitting up straight in the saddle, holding your reins up to your waist is the proper posture. You are talking to your horse as you did when you were walking with him. The trainer helping you at this point is there for you and the horse. You need to have that wonderful sense of the experience before you move any further. You will walk alone with the horse when you, the horse and the trainer feel you are ready.

Walking by yourself mounted on the back of your horse is an amazing feeling. You are up off the ground being carried by this wonderful animal and enjoying the moment. The connection you have established with your companion and best friend at this point makes you feel you and your horse have come full circle in your relationship. You have bonded and it shows.

The next test comes when you feel you and the horse can accomplish the next step; learning to ride. There is the walking with the horse, you have done this. Now it is breaking into a trot. This is where the horse begins to move with quick steps and you bounce. It is a good test to see if you can control yourself and hang on. I do not like the trot but it is necessary in learning to ride. You learn to control the horse and yourself. The goal is to try to become one with the horse. Move with the horse and not against him. If you can get comfortable with this step, the next step is easier.

The canter is going from the trot to a longer faster stride for the horse. I like this stride the best because you can find that meshing together with the horse and you become a part of each other. It is like a well oiled machine. You are moving with each other, not against. The motion of moving up and down as if you were rolling together. It is as if you were in a rocking chair going back and forth. The tempo is such that a rhythm is found. You are in the saddle and the horse in stride, moving as one. Just like rocking a baby. You and the horse can stay at this pace for a long time without tiring or getting sore in the saddle. The trot is more of a pounding sensation.

Finally, the gallop is the fastest you can go. A full gallop will challenge you to stay with the horse. You have to relax and let your body follow the horse. At this speed you need to be aware that the horse is in control. Just like riding a motorcycle, go with the speed. You do not want to change direction abruptly because unless you are an experienced rider you will probably go in a different direction. Consequently the horse and you can separate and you go flying off the horse. A seasoned rider will be able to anticipate a horse changing direction and be prepared to follow.

One of the best ways to learn to ride is bareback. I can remember getting up early in the morning with Robert and Kelly, going out to bring the horses in from the pasture. Kelly being a herding dog already has instincts as what to do. Actually we let her take over. We were there to assist.

While on the horse without a saddle you learn to give instructions with your body. You hold onto the mane to steady yourself and let the horse know what you want. You need good balance and control your stature with your knees. This also gives the horse direction. Lucky Jo and I had the kind of relationship which we could practically read each others minds. Much like being married for many years; learning enough about each other you can anticipate each others thoughts and actions.

Lucky Jo and I knew what to do, taking instruction from Kelly and Robert. It being early morning, the sun just rising, moisture hovering over the valley, the birds waking up to songs of joy and the smell in the air was as if you were walking through a flower shop or a nursery. The peace is unbelievably quite even with the horses coming in. This sound is joyful and it makes you feel as though you can do anything. The presence of God is so real and I can share that with my family. This is the closest to heaven on earth. What a wonderful cycle of life. God certainly has a plan that is right.

The horses pick up speed and we follow their lead. We break into a canter and Lucky Jo and I are working together. Becoming so attached to his feel, it is almost like riding by myself. His response to me is evident of love and concern because he knows enough how to take care of me on his back. Without the restriction of the saddle, the sensation of his muscular body working with mine feels as if anything could be accomplished. We are soul mates.

Our journey is over, reluctantly but there is always tomorrow. That is one thing so special about living on the ranch. Everything has to be done repetitively and that is fine with me. I love it all, even doing the things you may think are disgusting. Think of taking care of a baby. Some things are disgusting but you feel more for the baby than yourself. You think of the needs of the child and rescue as you should. How would you feel if it were you?

Special Needs Children

Another aspect of the Ranch is that my aunt and uncle open up the ranch for special needs children. It is proven that horseback riding is an excellent way to reach certain heeds and allows the children an opportunity to experience something they never thought they would or could.

We have children who are emotionally withdrawn from a trauma in their lives, those who are mentally challenged, and those that are physically challenged. Inside so many children they are just like us; they do not have the ability to express themselves. Some do not have the motor skills which make it possible for them to take care of themselves. It is amazing that the horses and the other animals do not even notice. They take everyone just as they are.

In most cases involving a number of people or animals, there are your favorites. You try not to show it but your heart reaches out to something familiar about them. You recognize a certain kind of pain or reaction that you identify with. You feel the connection and so do they. It is much like two people or animals drawn to each other. They all look alike but you sense something different in them. This draw is what brings you together. When the response is mutual, then it is twice as enjoyable.

One of the children that came to the ranch was Stephen. He is twelve years of age but part of him has not been able to mature like the rest of him. He is diagnosed as Autistic. "Autism is a physical disorder of the brain that causes a lifelong developmental disability. The many different symptoms of autism can occur by themselves or in combination with other conditions such as mental retardation, blindness, deafness, and epilepsy. Because children with autism – like all children- vary widely in their abilities and behavior, each symptom may appear differently in each child. For example, children with autism often exhibit some form of bizarre, repetitive behavior called *stereotyped behavior.*

Some of the symptoms of Autism are:
1. Failure to develop normal socialization
2. Disturbances in speech, language, and communication
3. Abnormal relationships to objects and events
4. Abnormal responses to sensory stimulation
5. Developmental delays and differences
6. Begins during infancy or childhood "

(From the book "Children with Autism – A Parents' Guide" edited by Michael d. Powers,

Psy. D., Woodbine House . 1989)

Some of Stephens's characteristics are that he shows no interest in making friends. He prefers his own company rather than being with others. He does avoid eye contact.

His communication skills are okay but he lacks the ability to pretend and has no real imagination. He will ask the same questions over and over even though you answer the question. His response to your questions may or may not be acknowledged. You just have to rely on body language; after knowing the child you begin to see a pattern that may be your communication level with him.

Stephen comes to the ranch regularly with the other children. Each child is assigned a horse with his or her adult who has come with them, to be on a one on one relationship. Each child needs the full concentration of the adult in charge. We prefer it not be the parent so we can work objectively. Some children need the parent for support and concentration. Each case is different.

I have taken a liking to Stephen. I have chosen to be his adult companion while he is here. I did feel a connection with him. It was not the usual outside interaction but the inside draw to one another, just like the feeling I have with my friends, my pets. The inability to show how he feels can be a guessing game. You just have to trust your instincts and see how well the two of you do get along. He is comfortable around me and he will listen to me.

When they arrive, he does come to me. He calls me Ms. Anita and that is perfect. Planning an agenda is good but it really is determined by the child for the day's events. My response is to ask him if there is anything he would like to do? If not, then I will take the lead.

When Stephen first came he was such a different child. He was shy and did not ask too much of anything. My place is to be around all the children but I kept coming back to Stephen. He would follow with the other children but more like a robot.

The first thing we did was to introduce them to the ranch. We took them for a wagon ride, with the hay and all the trimmings. Robert drove the wagon with the horses, and the children just observed. Amazingly they were not afraid. Their adult companion would explain things as we would drive around the ranch. They could see the few cows we had, the chicken coupe, the barn with the horses, and the horses in the pasture. The scenery is beautiful and the smells are sensational. It is not our judgment call to wonder how much they realized. Our job is to give them the experience. You do not look for a reward with these precious children, you just thank the Lord you can be a small part of their lives and bring something special to them. You cannot interpret what someone is thinking or feeling.

After the wagon ride we come back to the ranch. As the children are getting out of the wagon, getting help if they need it, Stephen climbed out and went to the barn. Following him to observe what he was going to do or wanted, making sure he was going to be safe was my thought. As he stood in the barn he was still and just looked around. He was silent but he was thinking. Watching with expectation and concern, he knew why he was there. Observing, I would just follow his lead.

As he started walking through the area where the stalls were, he was just looking around. It was mysterious watching him think and then move. Keeping by his side to keep him safe, passing by the horses stalls I could tell him about the horses. He had something in mind that was for sure but he could not communicate exactly what it was he was searching for.

Amazingly he stopped at Lucky Jo's stall and Fudzer happened to be in there with him. It was their afternoon chill out because morning on the ranch begins early. The gate to his stall was closed so we looked over it to see inside. Lucky Jo immediately responded to me and was excited to see me. It was interesting that Stephen was not afraid. Lucky Jo came and gave me a kiss and looked at Stephen with approval because he was with me. Stephen reached up and touched Lucky Jo on the nose. He was not afraid. Believe it or not, Stephen even looked into his eyes. This was a first for me. It was difficult for Stephen to make eye contact.

We stayed there for sometime enjoying Lucky Jo. Then Stephen heard Fudzer's meow and he wanted to know who or what it was. I called Fudzer to the ledge of the gate and she jumped up. Stephen was not startled at this either. It was as if he had all understanding as never before. This animal world he understood. The adult world is more confusing to him.

We spent more time with the two of them. I was in no hurry because my time was for Stephen and this is where he wanted to be. Then he pointed to the handle which indicated to me that he wanted to go inside with Lucky Jo and Fudzer. I asked Lucky Jo if it was alright and Fudzer gave her approval. Slowly opening the gate, we entered. He went over in the corner and sat down on the milking stool that Fudzer still sleeps under. As he sat there, Fudzer jumped up on his lap. He was so responsive, he actually started stroking Fudzer, she was purring, and Stephen loved the sound. Her coat is black and white long hair so she feels good and soft. He likes the way she felt. He even put her up to his face. He spoke to her and said her name.

As I am witnessing this unimaginable scene, a child coming out of his enclosed shell and showing something he has never done before. He was speaking to the animals and enjoying being with them. They responded as if they were glad he was there. He felt liked, as if he were at home.

With the help of Lucky Jo, I could help Stephen learn to ride. He did learn how to saddle and get the horse ready. This monumental event was a break through to immense proportion. His family was so thankful that they were able to see their son in what they considered happy. To them this was almost a first. Stephen usually did not respond as he has done with the animals.

When Stephen would come out to the ranch, I would find him in the barn with Lucky Jo and Fudzer. They welcomed his visits and Stephen took it upon himself to clean their stall, groom them and take care of them. That is all he wanted to do. Then as the reward after the work, he would ride for a while. I got to be a part of that. This was such a wonderful expression of God's love. Some of the simplest things in life mean so much to some and not to others. God loves us in a simple way and He wants you to come to him in a simple, humble way.

We saw the possibilities of what many would say were impossible. It depends upon your expectations and perspectives. With break through situation we saw, we knew we were doing what we were supposed to do.

CHAPTER 7: Horses to Ride / Horses to Roam

Horses Came with the Ranch

When I inherited the ranch, the set up that my uncle and Robert had decided would be, is the true meaning of the ranch. It is centered on horses. My passion is horses so there is no need to change with this comfortable setting.

The horses were used for many reasons. There were those that we would break for riding purposes and those we would keep for studding. Each one has his purpose but they all needed training. We could ride the stud horses if you were up to the challenge because of the nature of their use, they were pretty temperamental. If you wanted to know how good a rider you were, just take your challenge on one of them.

They were difficult to control especially, if they knew there was a breeding mare close by. He did not care who or what was on his back. He wanted the mare and that was it. Even a woman in her time of the month had to stay clear of the studding horse because he would want to mount her. There are a lot of natural things that human being need to be aware of. The horse is only acting upon instinct and that is why he is used to stud.

One horse in particular I was very fond of. He is a studding horse but he had an enjoyable personality. Believe it or not, he was gentle with me. Robert played a tremendous roll in getting this horse, which I named Blaze, to let me approach him and we could have a relationship. He would let me ride if he decided he wanted to. It was up to him rather riding was going to be alright. It must be a mood thing; that is where permission was needed.

While in the corral with Blaze we were having a good time. He would play tag, I would run after him and then he would run after me. Managing to get up on the fence a couple of times Blaze did win most of the time.

Blaze would even let Kelly into the corral as we played. Kelly did better playing with Blaze because of her herding skills. Kelly is so fast and her instincts are so capable of handling any situation. She is amazing.

Blaze is a young horse and soon he is getting taller. He is now about 15 hands high. He is turning into a beautiful red-brown color and has a manor about him that is so attractive. He is cocky but confident which is part of his charm. He is a tease which gives me an opportunity to return the jesters. Lucky Jo watches to see that I am okay. He will step in if he feels trouble. This watchful companion has been my security for as long as I can remember.

We were having a great time when Robert was working on the tractor and it back fired with a loud noise that sounded like a gun shot. Blaze was startled and felt threatened. All of the sudden he jumped the fence and took off running. A startled horse is one that is traveling so fast, it is difficult to catch. Fear takes over reason and escape seems to be the alternative.

Kelly immediately is in fast pursuit and then Lucky Jo. He knew instinctively Blaze could get in trouble being startled so suddenly. Kelly knew what she had to do when she caught up with him. How long would it take, we did not know, but we were afraid if he got to the back of the fenced area, he could jump that fence. My Uncle, Robert and I were in hot pursuit with the truck. More than anything we did not want any of the animals to get hurt.

Sure enough Blaze did jump the fence. Kelly and Lucky Jo knew enough with the training we have given them that they were not to follow. They have been trained to stay within the fenced area. As we got there they were waiting for us. We told them that they were good for not following. There was nothing we could do about Blaze. Our only hope is that he might find his way back. He may be threatened by the wild dogs or join the wild mustangs. I rode Lucky Jo home with Kelly at my side. My Uncle and Robert took the truck.

You have to be prepared to release your feelings for the animals because of the situation. You never know what role they will play and how long they will be with you. Some of the horses find their place at the ranch and become permanent fixtures. Blaze was one of those rare horses that you want to keep. After his studding days were over, he would be made into gilding for the purpose of riding. The training from studding to riding is substantial because the horse has to respect his rider and follow commands. If the horse was not able to be trained for domestic use, he would be auctioned of to another ranch. This is part of the cycle of life for the horse.

As Blaze jumped the fence and we were held in by the fence, all we could do is imagine what might happen to him. He is on his own now and we have to pray he will find his way home. It is up to him. From his point of view, the startling could have caused him to run frantically, not realizing what he was doing. Jumping the fenced seemed to be an alternative.

After he jumped the fence, he was in strange territory. We basically have the fenced area, which is so large, prepared so that it is safe for the animals to roam. The cows and the horses can get into trouble if the land is not surveyed for objects or holes which are open season for a broken leg. The area is a safe habitat for the animals. Beyond the fence, it is anyone's guess. Blaze started to slow down, realizing he had put quite a distance between him and the loud noise. I do not even know if he realized we were coming after him.

While nervous and stressed out, he began to compose himself. He looked around his surroundings and it was all unfamiliar. He did not recognize anything and probably did not know what to do. He thoughtfully watched as he got his bearings to figure out what he should do. He had keen senses and was smart. Would he make the right choice or decide to make it on his own? I do not know if he is aware of the dangers that are waiting for him out there.

The wild dogs must have been lurking in a hidden area out of sight. They saw the lonely horse and felt they were in power. This one horse could feed the entire pack. They are always looking for food. Blazes' instincts to danger were right on target. It did not take long for him to realize that he had a fight on his hands.

He was capable of taking on the dogs but when they circle their prey, the victim is at there mercy. Blaze began to back off, watching intently as the dogs began to surround him. He was looking for an out but he found none. As they approached closer with their familiar growl of death, Blaze could feel the pressure taunting him as his options were diminishing. He continued to back up but they did have him surrounded and there was not much he could do. He was not about to go down without a fight.

Thinking only of defending himself he whinnied as loud as he could. It was a fearful cry as the trapped animal he was. He began to try to trample the dogs but he was definitely out numbered. He could feel a terrible pain in his leg as the dogs began to tear at his flesh. His desperation was on his mind so the pain was redirected. He fought with everything he had.

Another shot rang out but this one seemed welcome. It caused the dogs to cease as they saw some of their own fall. They ran for shelter and Blaze was relieved that the attack had ended, hopefully for good. Behind the rifle shot came Chief and his son Ahoe. They were out hunting and could hear the sound of fear, barking dogs and a horse in trouble. They came as fast as they could so they could assess the situation and help if necessary.

They knew the horse was Blaze because coming to the ranch they have gotten to know all the horses. They figured out that Blaze was not supposed to be out there and was definitely in trouble. The dogs fled and Blaze was in a state of trauma. He was jittering and whelping as Chief and Ahoe came close. They knew enough not to rush the wounded horse so they used their voice to make the approach. Blaze must have recognized them because the sense he had at the moment was one of being rescued.

They began to gently rub the horse so they could make a determination of his injuries. He was able to stand but blood was running from his wounded legs. The intention of the dogs was to have the horses legs give out, bring him down, and then they would be the victor. Fortunately for Blaze he was still standing when his rescuers came.

Chief went to his saddle bags and got some ointment and bandages he always made a habit of taking out on hunting trips in case of a wounded animal or themselves. It was his "magic potion" that he had made this secret recipe. He was willing to share in any emergency but the combination he put together was his own. His knowledge of the earth and the healing powers grown by nature were part of his amazing heritage as an Indian. We learned so much from him.

Blaze was accommodating because he knew he was rescued. The wounds would not keep him from walking but they needed to make sure they could stop the bleeding. The ointment and the bandages did their job as they contained the bleeding. When they were comfortable that Blaze could travel they decided to take him to their place which is closer. He would not have to walk so far.

They could tend his wounds, make sure there would not be any infection and examine the depth of the wounds. They gently walked beside him as they walked their own horses. Most important is getting Blaze to focus on home and not the frightening attack. This will stay with him a long time. It may cause him too much trauma to be of value to the ranch. There will be no judgment call until we know. This is just a possibility.

The slow walk to Chief and Ahoe's place finally came to an end. It was dark and the sounds of the night became louder. You could hear the dogs howling in the far distance but Blaze still felt to respond with fear. He began to get jumpy and uncomfortable. His jesters were obvious of the fear he was feeling. All they could do was to reassure him.

They took him into the barn to treat his wounds. They would contact us in the morning but right now Blaze was the priority. They had to take care of him and could not wait to get us. We would have done the same thing. The horse is their priority.

Some liquid was given to Blaze for him to sleep while the wounds could be dressed. They had to go deep to see how badly the wounds penetrated and apply the medicine deep into the wounds which would clean and heal. Some stitches would be required because of his torn flesh. They did not know how injured he was because it would take time and they had to see how the healing would take place.

If a fever began then we would know there was infection and possibly fatal in the end. This is why they had to treat the horse as soon as possible. The big difference is the ointment and bandages applied out where the attack took place. Chief and Ahoe possibly will be attributed with saving his life as well as preventing infection from setting in.

In the morning we could hear and then see Chief and Ahoe coming up to the ranch. We were happy to see them but we did not know about Blaze as yet. They greeted us in their usual friendly greeting and then told us of the previous days happenings. They reassured us that they did what they could and the rest is up to Blaze. We knew that Blaze was in the best hands possible and if he were going to live and be okay it was because of their intervention. We were blessed that they showed up when they did. I choose to believe they were angels sent to rescue Blaze.

Letting my uncle know that I wanted to go to Blaze, he knew my heart and my need to be a part of his healing. My emotions when it comes to horses are quite extreme. Remembering the accident that Lucky Jo, Kelly, Fudzer and I had going to the fair that experience showed me that the animals responded emotionally. Blaze needs to be settled and comforted so he can heal totally. If something does go wrong at least I know my being there was the best that could be done.

We got to Chief's place and immediately we went to the barn. Cautiously entering, we did not want to frighten Blaze. Gently approaching, we could see he was down and still asleep. Going to his head, picking it up, and then placing it in my lap, my stroking him softly speaking to him, my belief is he could hear and sense me being there. Even if it did not matter to him, it did matter to me. This is what I had to do. Settling in for possibly a long time, I was prepared. My memory of what it was like for me in the hospital after a three day coma and the five week stay in the hospital, this is going to make a difference.

Stroking Blaze and talking to him, reminds me of the time like this with Lucky Jo. The memory is vivid; it is feeling like a repeat of the same. Fortunately Lucky Jo recovered with no repercussions. Deep inside his memory he probably still feels what he went through but putting time between then and now is the true healing.

In the calmness of the night, my eyes began to close. Gently falling to one side, sleep was upon me. Laying next to Blaze, we both were sound asleep. It was an unusual sensation because under normal circumstances he probably would not let me. His nature is aggressive which is necessary for the role he plays in studding. This is not the Blaze we know. This is a wounded horse vulnerable and dependent on us for help.

We believe in him and we are willing to do whatever it takes to heal him. We even have to be prepared for the worst possible scenario. We might have to put him down if he cannot recover. You try not to think about it but on the ranch you may, not often, have to do what is best for the animal. This is why you do not try to get too close to the animals unless in the case of Lucky Jo, Kelly and Fudzer, they are meant to be pets. I need to be close to them but not break their spirit to do their job at the ranch.

Waking up in the morning, looking at Blaze his eyes were beginning to open. He did not try to get up; he knew I was there. In his own sense of awareness, he felt the comfort given by me. Beginning to talk to him telling him he is going to be alright, I could hear voices that were familiar. Chief, Ahoe, Princess, Ahoe's sister, and my uncle were glad to see us and wanted to know about the wounds that Blaze sustained.

As they examined him, unraveling his bandages, looking close to the wounds, they could see how deep they were. They needed to get Blaze up to see if he could stand on his legs or were they too badly damaged. If there was muscle damage, there was real cause for concern. We left Chief and Uncle Nick to the task at hand. They did not need us in the way.

As they talked to Blaze they did explain what they needed to do. They needed him to understand how important it was for him to be able to do this. Blaze had to do this on his own. He could not get help. He was too big and if he did not fight to get up he would have to be put down. This is such a critical time in the healing process.

Blaze did struggle to get up. It seems that the leg he uses the most to get up is wounded the worse. His balance was off and the struggle was not enough. He fell back down on his side. He could not muster up enough strength to bring himself up. This was not a good sign. My heart sank.

My desire was to go into the stall and talk to Blaze. He wanted to get up because of the fight in him. His weakened state prohibited him from being able to accomplish this. He lay there in his stall, defeated and surely hurting physically. This was such a difficult situation and life threatening. The wounds may not kill him but the inability to get up could.

I knelt down next to Blaze and began to talk to him. As the words came out they were to give him the strength to do this. Whatever he did he had to know we would be there for him. He needed a reason to struggle so the reminders of the good times we had together could be what he needed to hear. One of the reasons were that he has so much to live for but if he chooses to lie down and die, it was up to him.

Continuing to stroke him, there was a response as if to say get out of my way so I can get up. His muscles were beginning to tighten up, his head raised up and I backed up. Still talking to him but now it was a commanding voice. He needed the courage to do what he had to do and do it. His struggle was evident of the courage to reach his goal. He made noises and nays and finally figured out how to get up to compensate for the wounded leg that would not support him. He got to the point that if he gave one more push and pull on his body the weight shift and its momentum would bring him upright. Sure enough, the success of the feet was completed and Blaze is on all four's. Praising him, hugging him and telling him we were so happy for the choice he made.

Blaze did let my uncle and Chief examine him now that he was standing. They encouraged him to walk so they could see if he would favor one leg over another. From what they could tell at this point he was going to be alright. It was Chief's magic potion out on the range when Blaze was first wounded by the dogs saved his life.

We let Blaze stay at Chief's place but we made daily trips with Lucky Jo and Kelly. Everyday he seemed to be getting better. Walking him around to give him strength was good also it let him know we were there for him. We all need nursing care in one way or another. When my accident happened, my aunt was there for me thankfully. This is one of the greatest acts of love to participate in the healing and recovery of a loved one.

We did not know if Blaze could continue as a stud horse because his legs may not be strong enough to mount a mare in heat. It would take a while before we would know. His options were many if his studding days were over.

He could become a gilding and be a wonderful riding horse for the kids that visit the ranch. Even a wonderful riding pet if someone wanted to buy him for their own. Regardless of his future he has so much life still in him. He would not be discarded as useless but just play a different role at the ranch. He will be valuable and a treasure for the strength and courage he displayed to want to live. We knew then that he was destined for great things no matter how others may see the role he will play.

It had been a couple of weeks since the attack and Blaze was recovering so well. Chief was amazed at the healing of his wounds and the strength he was displaying. Chief felt that we could take him back to the ranch in about a week or so. He had to be able to make the trip walking on his own. We would be there for him but he had to do the walking himself.

The day arrived and Blaze was able to go home. We would not know if he could stud or not as yet but he could come home with us. He started acting his usual self, spunky, frisky and playful. The trip home was not the time to play but he could not help himself. He was like an encaged child ready to have fun. Confinement was against his nature. It has been a long time in his mind that he has been able to run and feel free. The problem was that we did not want his newly healed legs to be stressed causing further injury. Chief did give us some herbs that would calm him down for the journey home. This is necessary for his own good; much like sedating your pet for a trip. It relaxes them but they can still function and do what they have to do.

We arrive at the ranch and the familiar surroundings cause Blaze to respond in a way that made us all feel good.

You could tell he was happy to be home. He went to his stall to see if it was still there for him. His friends welcomed him and Robert played a tremendous part in his homecoming. He was able to rub him down as if to give him a massage which Blaze remembers the tender loving care and hands of Robert.

We left the two of them alone so Blaze did not get too excited his first night home. You could tell that Blaze was tired from the trip so the rest of the evening was calm and relaxing. Robert did bed him down, cover him with his familiar blanket, gave him his regular feed and water if he needed it. His stall was clean and ready for him.

In the morning upon awakening, my first priority is to see if Blaze is alright. Reaching his stall it was empty. Looking around for Lucky Jo he was not in his stall either. Coming out of the barn what did I see? Blaze, Lucky Jo, Kelly and Fudzer on the fence, all together as a family. When Robert got up he heard Blaze and Lucky Jo stirring in their stalls. As he approached them he could sense them becoming restless. He thought if he put them in the corral they may feel better. Of course Kelly was right there. She gets up at the crack of dawn with Robert. Likewise Fudzer follows with their lead.

Putting them in the corral is what they wanted. It was almost like children climbing in bed with their parents. The closeness of being intimate in a special way, Blaze could bond with Lucky Jo, Kelly and Fudzer. The picture in my mind of seeing them like this made me feel like a mother having her grown children coming home for the holidays. The memories you carry for a lifetime become a part of who you are as a person. We are actually a combination of our parents, our experiences and our memories.

As the days passed, Blaze continued to improve. My uncle and Robert were not sure of his future. They needed time to assess his progress. He began his ritual of play and promise but the strength in his legs was not improving as much as they would like. They started feeling that his studding days are over. This does not mean that he will not still be valuable to the ranch but his role will change.

The decision was made to make him gilding. This will temper him and he will be much calmer and gentle. He will be a wonderful riding horse for those who came to the ranch. Also, Lucky Jo, Kelly, and Fudzer had some influence on the decision to keep him. He also was a part of the family nursing him to health. How could we ever let him go?

Horses at Auction

One part of the business of the ranch is to take horses to the auction to make money. They were horses raised and trained for just that purpose. These horses you do not get attached to emotionally because they are meant for someone else and good stock and breeding. You treat them with respect and teach them to be good horses when they do go to auction. They are usually around two years old when the training begins so they follow instructions, are prepared for breeding and any other roles their owner may have for them.

I liked going with my uncle and Robert to the auction so I could see all the horses. We may even bid on a horse or two, depending if we think the horse will be an asset to the ranch. It would be a special horse with great potential.

As we unloaded our horses, four by number, we took them to a designated corral. We had to keep the horses separate from the others. You never know if one or more of them may decide to object to another horse; it would be dangerous as well as chaos. We unloaded our horses and settled them in. We would be called by number to display each horse for a potential buyer. Our ranch had a good reputation for excellent horses. This was in our favor.

Looking around at the other horses, my eye spotted a pure black mare that was stunning. She held her head high and her tail out. Her posture and demeanor were her greatest attribute. Her age would be estimated about two years of age. Approaching the corral she was being held in, our eyes made contact. It was as if they were pools of deep water swallowing me up. She did not try to free herself from my stare feeling we were communicating.

It was an emotional connection even though we have never met. Holding onto her focused glare which continued until I reached the corral. She then came toward me while I was climbing up onto the railing. Introducing myself, she responded very friendly. There was no fear just a sense of belonging. My experience told me this horse belonged with us and the ranch. She would be a wonderful asset to the ranch. We needed to bid on her. I have to let my uncle know so with his permission, we would bid on her for our own.

I left her to find my uncle. He and Robert were scanning all the horses available to see if they saw a horse they wanted to bid on. Telling them about the midnight mare I expressed my feelings toward the horse. They trusted my instincts and they were willing to look at her.

We found her and they began to asset her as a potential horse for the ranch. They knew what a horse should be but they have to decide if she fits into the criteria of the purposes of the ranch. The horse again fixed her eyes on me as if to say she was happy to see me. This is the first time she had been at an auction. She does not know if she realizes she may go to a new home. Regardless, I was praying that my uncle and Robert would want to bring her home.

As they examined her, found out her history and breeding, saw my anxious anticipation, they decided they did want her for our ranch. I was elated but the next step in her becoming ours is to bid her into our hands. Our horses were being favorably responded to and bid upon. All four of them were auctioned off and found a good home. Now we waited for our black beauty to come to the platform so we can bid for her.

As she came to the platform she was even more beautiful that ever. Remembering Lucky Jo and how my feelings were about him. He was special and so is she. Still praying that she would come home with us, the bidding began. It was a tug of war back and forth. My uncle knew what a good fair bid was. He has a limit and he usually sticks to that. We were at that limit when my heart sank. It is too late. We lost our beautiful horse. Unable to watch any longer, I retrieved to the truck. It was too painful to watch.

Not knowing how long it had been, the voice of my uncle and Robert were audible as they came to the truck. They knew how I felt about the horse and this missed opportunity was difficult for me. These things happen and you just have to learn how to get on with what is at hand.

My uncle asked for my help and reluctantly I agreed. He wanted some help getting a horse into the trailer. They did find a horse but being a bit disheartened, I did agree. Getting out of the truck and looking up, "My Black Beauty" is the horse needing help getting in the truck. Taken by such a surprise, my uncle smiled as did Robert. Whatever made him change his tactics did not matter, I was thrilled. My prayers were answered.

Later Robert told me that my uncle held out for the horse because she meant so much to me. Holding this secret close to my heart is one of the many treasured moments I have to remember my uncle.

Keeping the name Black Beauty for her is perfect; it suited her so well. I know it is not original but works for her. We got her home and put her in the corral. We have to keep her separate from the other horses at first. Getting to know her, train her to the rules of the ranch and then decide when she should have a foal. We will impregnate her when we feel she is ready.

We have the perfect male for her if she decides she wants him. It can be tricky but nature has a way of winning. Usually the best thing to do at that time is just let the two of them together when she is in heat and that's it. She wants it and he is happy to oblige. That is what she is there for and that is his role. A great combination plus it increases our own livestock. The life cycle of a ranch is becoming the part of that purpose.

The training begins for Beauty introducing her to my family. They watch as the first introduction is to Lucky Jo who trusts my judgment. Then Kelly approves, Fudzer is enjoying the new addition and Blaze is also consumed with the new family member. He is not interested in her as a companion. He has no desire for her to mate but looks to her as a friend as do the others. They watch as the process begins and she responds very well. Robert is so good at training the horses and I have learned so much from him. He saddles her and begins the routine of commands that she has to follow. She is excellent in her response and a quick learner. She is a wonderful horse.

Her training is over and I have the privilege of taking her riding out over the ranch. I take Lucky Jo and Kelly with me for help. She has to be disciplined and aware that I am on her back. If something startles her, she needs to handle the situation without fear and retreat. She has to confront her fear and then if running is the best option, she has to let me know her intentions or let me take command. She is not terribly large so she is easier to handle. Lucky Jo is taller and stronger but she is young and fast. Her training begins by going into the area away from the ranch. We are explorers on a journey to find treasure. Well at least it did sound good.

It was a beautiful day so the weather would not be an issue. Our journey is uneventful as far as anything to cope with so we can relax and enjoy the scenery. Beauty is behaving wonderfully and I am beginning to relax. This journey we are on is a pleasant experience. Talking to Lucky Jo, Kelly and Beauty, we are having a great conversation. The atmosphere is one of control and nothing to concern ourselves with. We must have been gone about one hour and we were approaching an area that had concealed brush keeping our view concealed.

Lucky Jo started to feel uncomfortable. Trusting his instincts explicitly, Beauty began to react and my first reaction. In the hidden area was something we were going to have to deal with. Kelly bravely approached the area and started barking. All of the sudden we could hear the rattles of snakes sounding like an orchestra. The problem was that they were life threatening. Lucky Jo backed off but Beauty did react to the snakes. She rose up in fear and began to tremble, then taking off and running.

Fortunately being an experienced rider, staying with her was more than just a fast run. This is an out of control run that you cannot stop her. Trying to anticipate her moves, riding this out was the best thing to do. We made it to the back fence and then over she jumped. My thoughts were that possibly she was going to suddenly stop and send me flying. Going over with her was the best for me.

We flew over the fence together and we made it. She was tiring out so talking to her was the best. Somehow she trusted my voice and began to feel a sense of the fear leaving. She started to slow down and bring herself under control. Pulling back on the reins, this is telling her to stop. She followed her instincts and her training. We were coming into a sensible gait and now she was beginning to halt. Continuing to pull on the reins, she did stop. I dismounted to let her know everything was all right and the danger is gone.

Beauty was panting profusely so my rubbing her and talking to her was helping. Taking the reins we started walking back. After she settled down I would mount her again and find Lucky Jo and Kelly. Hopefully they were at the fence but did not jump over as we did. They should be waiting for us there.

Beauty began to settle down and her breathing was telling me that she was doing better. Her heartbeat was slowing down also from the frightening incident. Fortunately she did not get bitten by the snakes. This is one predator that horses do have to fear. Beauty has learned her first lesson about the dangers of hidden snakes.

As we continued walking we could see the fence and yes, Lucky Jo and Kelly were on the other side. As we got closer they both showed their happiness that we were okay. As they danced around and whinnied and barked this told me exactly what they were thinking. We got to the fence and Beauty responded also with pleasure to see them. We were all so happy that everyone is alright.

After our little reunion the problem exists to get Beauty over the fence. This being her first outing out for training the question is can she jump the fence again? The first time was natural instinct of survival. This time it is a conscious attempt to jump the fence at will. Would she see it as impossible, a challenge but I want to try or would she see it for what it was; the need to jump to get us over the fence so we can join Lucky Jo and Kelly and back to the ranch.

Speaking to her I told her what had to be done. She had to jump the fence so we could get on the other side. Mounting on her back, she had to back up a way so we could get a running start. She knew this and was obedient. Doubt did come to my mind but believing in her was what she needed of me. I am trusting that she can.

Her character and determination gave me the confidence she is going to make it. My prayers are she will make it and be the horse I already know she is. We are now in place and with the signal to go she starts running. She breaks into a gallop and without hesitation we fly over the fence and onto the other side. She was amazing and we have a jumper on our hands. Certain horses are born with certain characteristics. Some horses are jumpers, some are race horses and some are companion horses. Just like people. We are all born or bred into something with a special potential.

Lucky Jo and Kelly were so happy to see us and we all headed back to the ranch. Anxious to report our trip and the discovery about Beauty as a jumper, is exciting. If her potential is realized she will be a valuable asset to the ranch. She will be a wonderful horse for someone who wants to jump horses and possibly in competition. This could be a great option and valuable to the credentials of the ranch. The more variety there is to the ranch the better the reputation for an outstanding ranch.

Horses Run Wild and Majestic

The horses running wild on the property was such an addition to the character of the ranch. As they would appear and disappear, they would remind us of the freedom existing inside all of us.

In maintaining this freedom, we want to make certain these horses can be free to do what comes natural to them. We briefly monitor them to see if they are well or need our assistance. Occasionally a horse in is danger needing some medical attention. As we isolate the horse from the herd, we deal with the illness.

It may be a thorn in its hoof or a wound from scrapping against something. It does not take much but it will be very serious if left unattended.

When we know the horses are coming around the perimeter of the ranch, we make ourselves available to lasso a horse in trouble so we can take care of the need. The other horses continue to run and they seem to know the routine. This is an annual event which almost becomes time sensitive. We can count on the run coming soon.

While observing with a watchful eye, a sound of thunder permeates the air. We know what to expect and we are ready to respond. We have our mounted horses ready to join the run and watch if we can see a horse in trouble.

The sound is almost deafening and our horses are anxious to join the run. As the wild horses reach the fence they naturally veer off in perfect timing. We start running to catch up to their pace. Inside the herd we can view all the horses. We pull forward or drop back to overlook the herd. Usually the ailing horse or horses are to the back.

Robert and my uncle spotted a horse in need. They began their game plan to isolate the horse so he can be roped. This is very difficult but both my uncle and Robert are well experienced and usually successful.

Their attempt at first try is accomplished. They were able to slow the running horse down so they could examine it. They had to wait for the other horses to pass and deal with a horse that did not want to be caught.

Another horse was found and brought to the same area for examination. We included chief in on this part of the ranch chores because he is so wonderful with horses and the healing that is needed.

The first horse had torn flesh hanging from its side. Blood was dried and some still oozing. This called for medicine and stitches. How to get this wild horse under control was difficult but not impossible. Chief has come equipped with his wonder drug for sedating the horse. This would not be possible otherwise.

We needed to get the horse to slow down long enough so it would inhale the poignant fumes that would put the horse down so we could work on it. We worked simultaneously with the other horse. It was better to do them at the same time.

As we examined the second horse, we could see that there was something caught in his gum and something in his leg. Both were beginning to fester which means infection. If this is not taken care of the horse will die, it is simple as that.

As both horses are down, we take care of them with the knowledge and experience we have. Occasionally we have to call upon the vet but most of the time we do it ourselves. There usually is not time for the vet to reach the sick or injured horse.

We were successful in attending to the injured horses. We put medicine after removing what needed to be eliminated. The heavy suave would keep the area clean and the medicine in the mouth after removing the object will be sufficient. The horse's salvia will keep the wound clean.

The horses were coming around after the sedation worked itself off. They were a bit groggy but were coming to life. They had a sense of knowing all was fine because the pain from the wounds had subsided. The experience they had was they felt better. They have a sense of knowing all is well.

They began on their journey to join the herd. I expected that they would take off in a flash. It was interesting to see them begin to run, they stopped to look back as if to say thank you, and returned to seeking their family.

We are thankful for the opportunity that we can help so we can keep the balance of the ranch intact. Caring for the wild animals is a part of the environment of the ranch and we want to do what we can to preserve its integrity. The running of the horses is so majestic and awesome that if it were to stop so much would be lost.

CHAPTER 8: Rehabilitating Horses

Race Horses

Another aspect of the ranch which is such a part of me is the opportunity we have to help horses that are hurt or in trouble. They come to the ranch for help and to recuperate. A lot of the time horses just need time to recover in an atmosphere for healing and therapy.

Race horses are born and bred to race. It is part of their nature. To run is to live and to live is to be a race horse. When a horse has reached the end of his career there are a few choices. The choice is usually studding for the male or breeding a mare.

We had a mare arriving that was just in that category. Her last race cost her ability to run anymore but her reputation as an excellent runner made her valuable. She was to be bred so she could produce a foal of high quality.

The owner has the choice to keep the foal for himself or sell her when she is about two years old to be trained as a racer. A lot depends upon the development of the foal as time goes on.

A compatible male was sent with her so the two could breed. To keep the blood line pure it is important that she not be contaminated by another horse. Part of the process of breeding is to continue the blood line as pure as possible. She has to be protected at all times.

The two horses were let loose in a contained area so they could run and play and as the moment was right, she was agreeable, she would give her permission for him to mount her. Of course the male followed her lead as most men do. It did not take long and she was impregnated. The owners decided to leave the two of them on our ranch for a while so she could have a good beginning for her foal while developing. The male did stay attached while they resided at the ranch.

Injured Horses

We have had a lot of experience with injured horses with our own. Part of the job of the healing is to understand the emotional needs of the horse. They are no different from other animal or people when they have to arrive above a traumatic experience. This is the part I like because of my understanding of horses.

We had another horse arriving that was hit by a truck. It was one of those unfortunate moments that no one was really to blame. It could have been avoided but this is why they called it an accident.

The horse was startled and began to run. He ran across a road which unfortunately had a truck moving down the road. When the horse realized and the driver saw the horse, it was too late. They collided and both were damaged.

The driver was injured because the impact was so sudden; it took a while for him to regain consciousness and to be rescued. The horse lay still and the question is will he still be alive and if so, how badly injured? Help did arrive because witnesses saw what happened and took immediate action. Some helped the driver and the others attended to the horse.

The driver broke his arm being thrown against the steering wheel. The seat belt kept him from flying into the windshield. His ribs will be sore but the seat belted did a great job of keeping the injuries from being more severe.

From what we understand is that the horse had internal injuries but not too severe. It seems that his emotional state is what is in jeopardy. This is why he has been brought to the ranch.

This was going to be a job for all my friends. Lucky Jo, Kelly, Fudzer and Blaze all had a different role to play. Companionship is probably the best medicine right now. The horse is skittish so we will take it easy.

The animals seemed to sense what the horse needed. They knew when to be there and when to back off. Eventually they were found hanging out together. The horse was able to focus on other things rather than himself. The wounds were healing faster than the emotional state of his mind. This was going to be a long journey but the owner believes he is worth it.

Emotionally Disturbed Horses

There are times when a horse is very emotionally distraught. It could be from an experience to overwhelming to get past or by excessive abuse. There are those horses that have been mishandled or starved. It does not take much to have these kinds of trauma's affecting the life of a horse.

One of the horses brought to us was just such a case. The abuse had gone on for a long time. You did not realize what the horse was living in and through until the authorities got involved. The owner was having a terrible time in his own life and he was taking it out on the horse.

The horse belongs to his wife and the difficulty in the home had to do with the marriage. He was abusive to his wife but it did not stop there. He continued even more aggressively with the horse. Whether it was a strap at hand or an instrument to inflict pain, this was his choice of weapon.

Fortunately for the horse, he was able to run free in the pasture. He did have to come home occasionally to feed on oats and water. At times the rancher would lock the gate so the horse was abandoned for days. Even in inclement weather the horse had to find his own shelter.

A neighbor had an opportunity to see the abuse of the wife and then the horse first hand. In a fit of rage, he struck his wife causing her death. Still in a mood of such anger, he turned on the horse. The horse was able to retreat for protection. The enraged rancher found gasoline and proceeded to put the ranch on fire.

When the authorities finalized all the necessary investigation and paperwork, the neighbor was able to round up the horse, bring him to us and it was up to us to determine if the horse could be rehabilitated or had to be destroyed.

When the horse arrived I knew the story about the horse. I knew the damage that surrounded him and it would take time to assess the prognosis on the future of the horse.

At first the best thing to do was to let him alone. He was fearful at our handling so we had to be cautious in our attempts to care for him. The atmosphere at the ranch was quite peaceful considering we had so much going on.

I was going to give the horse a name. As I looked at the horse I could see potential underneath the veneer of abuse. He had cuts and bruises with harden clay on his body. His feet were neglected where his hoofs were causing him to walk with a limp. His eyes were cloudy and the life had gone out of them. His mane and tail were full of briers because no one was grooming him. He hung his head in a down position just as someone would be living as he was.

Looking at the horse what came to mind was Hope. This name may help the horse learn to trust and then be able to contribute. This may be the incentive to struggle to get better. Surrounding the horse with a lot of hope would give him a sense of security he probably has never had.

As the days passed by Hope began to realize that we were not going to treat him badly. We approached him with caution simply because he did not startle well. He was constantly on the defensive. This was going to change.

Lucky Jo played the most important role to Hope. When we let Hope out into the corral, we would have Lucky Jo in there also. Kelly was right behind and of course, Fudzer on the fence. Blaze would occasionally join in. They invited Hope to play but I do not think he knew how to be a horse.

There is a lot of enjoyment taking care of Hope. Talking to him with a voice of sincerity, he could feel comfort as did my other friends. We were going to see if it would be possible to saddle him for riding. This may be an obstacle that he could not overcome. His mistrust could be greater than his ability to trust someone on his back.

With my uncles permission and the opinion of Robert, I asked if they thought Hope was ready. Chief had dropped by to see the horse and he thought this was as good a time as any. I was confident that it was the right time also. There is tremendous support and help surrounding me. All were watching but trying to keep Hope from seeing this. We did not want to scare him needlessly and he should concentrate on the two of us.

Hope was used to the bridle. Brushing him and getting him ready for me to put the blanket on his back, his tail and mane helped to keep the blanket to stay in place. Gradually I introduced the saddle to him. He looked at it and then he looked at me as if to say it was okay. I took his look as a yes and proceeded to put the saddle on his back. Grabbing the cinch to bring it under his belly would secure the saddle. Tightening the cinch so the saddle would not fall off, this is important while trying to mount on his back. Proceeding to walk with Hope, Lucky Jo followed. As we got close to the railing of the fence, climbing up would help me to get on Hope's back. The fence gave me a more secure hold while swinging my leg over.

Predictably Hope began to rise up in discontent. He did not like the saddle. He continued to rear up to get me off. He tried to get me off his back but I was determined to stay put. It was a matter of wills at this point. The survival of the fittest lasted a couple of minutes. As he tried to end this in his way, determination to the end is my way. He has to trust me or he will be of no value to the ranch.

It is now payday. Either he starts to earn his keep or we have to destroy him. He will not be able to be totally healed for him to be an asset to the ranch. We have to at least be able to ride him.

Feeling his body start to relax and the intensity is beginning to subside, staying with his movements is important. Eventually he will have to come to a halt so I can dismount him. Also I have to be able to mount him again without his objections.

He is coming to a halt and he is quieting down. He does know it is me on his back. The trust and bond is beginning to form so we can mold him into the horse that will be valuable. It is up to him now.

I was able to get off his back while holding the reins in my hands. His reaction as he looked into my eyes, he sought out the approval he had always been denied. After that day he was a beautiful horse the children could ride..

CHAPTER 9: Camping in the Mountains

The Requirements

In the summer we plan on the camping experience of the year. Those who qualify have the adventure of a lifetime. It is not only unforgettable but it can be life changing.

Money is not one of the requirements. You could pay one million dollars and it would not make a difference. The necessary requirement is to think of your camping mates before yourself. You need to be equipped with knowledge of camping and have been experienced sleeping, climbing and cooking in the wild. Learning to eat what is around you and know how to survive if you are lost is a must. Anything less is not acceptable.

Usually those picked to take this journey are brought to us as a referral. It usually is someone who knows someone, etc., type of scenario. The desire to contribute has to be more than what can I get out of it? We will pick a mix of different types because everyone has something to offer.

Robert, me, Ahoe and Princess were to be the guides. Ahoe and Robert would handle the things that Princess and I could not. We all have a good working relationship so we can think for each other.

The age was about sixteen to twenty-five. The maturity level and how they are living life now is critical. One of the girls is sixteen but she is used to working her parent's ranch, taking care of her mother and younger siblings, going to school. Her maturity level is much better because she has accepted her role without complaining. We wanted her to be able to go because she deserved it and she would be a good influence to the other girls. They have to be tough, not unfeminine.

Learning so much from my Indian heritage and from Robert, my uncle, Chief, Ahoe and Princess. They would honor the woman in me but challenged me as a person in survival or complicated situations. A great experience is learning the "how to" when it came to my animals. A lot of it was on-the-job training.

Hard work has always been a part of my personality. I've never been afraid or neglectful when it came to getting things done. Personally tackling the job sooner than later is my philosophy so it is behind me.

Basic Training

We assemble all the candidates two weeks before we set out on our journey of exploration. They are looking forward to the exploration but in the back of their minds they want to see what they are made of in difficult situations. Can I survive on my own knowledge or do I have to depend on someone else? These are important questions the kids are asking themselves. Their thought process is in contributing not receiving. Most kids want to know what is in it for them. This is the maturity level we want to demonstrate.

The basic training is setting up tents, cooking, cleaning up and then clean yourself before we even set out. They need to know how to handle the basic necessities such as a knife, cooking utensils, washing, and other housekeeping rules. They needed to have each one know his or her horse so that they would be dependent on each other. Both their lives may depend on it and how to get each other home.

Knowing how much they knew about the sky, the stars, reading the clouds, and watching out for signals around them, is important. Another important lesson is to know about dangerous plants, good plants, medicine plants as well as the water. The use of trees can save your life in the right situation that should come our way.

Basic training was just that; a basic knowledge of fitness and survival to help yourself or your partners in time of trouble or fun. Getting to know each other before moving out is so important so they can learn to start trusting one another. The time may come when this is a reality and you had better know you may have to trust someone with your life.

One of the techniques we had to learn was that of climbing. We had some awesome trees that were happy to volunteer. The barn was also a good example of maneuvering on ropes in the air. The straw below was a great barrier to fall on if you were in trouble, even though there would not be the soft landing on our trip. It is a good confidence booster in the training process.

Fishing and canoeing in the stream was good training also. We would be carrying canoes, alternating with each other. There would be times we would secure the horses at a designated area where canoes were stored. We could venture out into the canoe, fish, and whatever, come back to the horses and continue on. We did have to pack wet weather gear for just those days that the clouds decided to unload the water stored in them.

Assigned a Horse

Interestingly, this was one of the easiest parts. Each student and each horse seemed to search out each other. It was over several days of boot camp that this was done. They all had a chance to meet and ride any of the designated horses for the trip.

One student did not have a lot of experience with horses. She was familiar with dogs and had her favorites. Horses were not in her life as much as the other students. She showed apprehension and a bit of fear when it came to the horses. She would even shy away as we approached the horses.

One day Princess saw what was going on with this particular student. She could sense the struggle instead of her. Princess was sensitive to this for both her and the horse. She knew how both were feeling.

One of the horses is a quarter-horse that has a background of being handled by kids. The parents realized that the children needed to be taught how to behave with the horse and the horse needed to learn how to tolerate the kids. The horses name was Georgia and she had a wonderful personality and was able to tolerate and teach the kids. She is now up in years, those children are now grow up and we have Her to be a part of our ranch and what we are doing.

Georgia must have sensed the intimidation from the student. While at the ranch, the horses were free to roam in certain areas. The students could go up to the horses anytime and ride. This is how they were going to make their choice of what horse they wanted for the camping trip.

The student, Susan, would go near the corral but stand her distance. She wanted to go closer but was afraid of the horses. She did not know what to expect or what she should do. She needed time to experience and watch the other students and how they handle themselves.

One day Susan came up to the fence to watch the horses. She was looking at them but I do not know if she knew how to really look at the horses. The meaning to this is in complete eye contact from both the human and the horse. The commitment of the moment acknowledged by the presence of each other and their existence being real and attached.

Susan had climbed up on the fence which was a first for her. She could sense someone looking at her. It was not an uncomfortable feeling just a sense of vulnerability. Her eyes scanned over the horses and her eyes met this horse Georgia. She stayed focused on her eyes as did Georgia on Susan's eyes.

She was not self-conscious but taken by the trance she was caught in. As she held the glare into Georgia's eyes, she began coming up to Susan. A bit frightened but not ready to move away, she waited to see what would happen. As Georgia came closer she moved next to the fence so Susan could touch her. Susan responded and then moved to Georgia's mane and head. Susan even got to her nose and talked to her. Georgia moved her head so she could look at Susan and she responded. The connection was made.

After that Susan sought out Georgia as did Georgia seek out her, which made them partners. We could get her riding and comfortable before we leave on our trip. This was a more dramatic bonding but much the same with each student and horse.

Preparing the Food and Supplies

Cooking was one thing but learning to cook over an open fire is another. We needed to show them how to cook certain foods and how to prepare them without all the condiments they are used to. Food does not have to taste bad in this type of a situation but there are ways to add natural herbs that can be found in the woods.

We showed them how to dry beef, preserve certain things, smoke fish all which were able to be pack or stored.

We took salt and a few things we could use for first aide such as baking soda, etc. Flour was good for biscuits and of course beans. We packed lard instead of oil or butter. We packed canteens for water, sleeping bags, tents, lanterns, matches, and a compass for each one. Water purifier for water that was questionable to drink. Each student has there own mess kit they were responsible for. A hat and extra socks to keep feet dry. A portable shovel, axe, knife, line and hooks for catching fish, pliers, which should take care of any emergency. They did have a GPS attached to each students shoe in case someone got lost, separated, or in danger.

The last thing was the campfire. In this time of boot camp and learning, a fire is essential. They learned how to gather the right kind of wood, what was good for kindling, and how to start a fire without matches. Hopefully the matches would continue to be available but all it would take would be a down pour of rain and everyone's matches got wet. We do not think that all would but what if this worse case scenario became a reality. They are all depending on each other for survival. Together they have a better chance with everyone pulling together their resources then one alone.

Graduation day has arrived, the students have passed all their requirements and they are ready and excited to put to task what they have learned. They are anxious for the experience and spending time with their new found friends.

We have made it clear that there is to be no relationship development on this trip because the focus has to stay on each other and what needs to be done. There is no difference between the males and females when it comes to work, chores or whatever. Only in matters where the male is stronger and a female cannot. Otherwise there is no respecter of persons. All are accountable to each other the same.

The Camping Trip

The time has come for the trip to begin. We are confident that the group we have is excited and confident for the journey and challenges ahead. There are no guarantees but the education gives them the tools to act and perform in any situation.

We are headed for the mountains. It will take about one days walking to get there. The weather is beautiful, our horses and each student are packed, and we are ready to head out. I have Lucky Jo and Kelly with me because of their experience I can trust them with my life and the life of anyone of the students.

Robert, Ahoe, Princess and I all have charge of four students each. There are sixteen students in all, eight boys and eight girls. Princess and I have the girls and Robert and Ahoe have the boys. The students can relate better to each of us.

As we made our way toward the mountain we can see the ranch disappearing. We began to climb upwards a bit so as we looked back the ranch was getting smaller. Home was becoming less significant and the road ahead more prominent. The excitement in me is arising as on all the camping trips because the anticipation of this trip will change the lives of the students forever.

We reach the base of the mountain, unpack, set up camp and remark at what a wonderful trip that day. We had set up a routine of rotating the chores so everyone knew what their job was and expected to do it. No complaints were allowed because we knew it was going to get much more difficult as we got farther into our journey.

If they wanted to complain that was okay but not out loud or to another student. If they were asked to do something "No" was not an option. If they did not like the way things were they had to keep it quiet, bare the feelings and bit the bullet. You do as you are told or expected to react. Acceptance is the only thing option.

The pre-training really paid off this first night. All tents went up, dinner cooked, clean-up of camp and self and all lights out for the early morning start. Sun up was the hour to get up; breakfast, clean-up and we are ready for day two.

The joy throughout the camp is exhilarating and I pray it continues no matter what comes our way. We did take time to pray before going out and at night thanking God for the safe journey of the day past and a safe one for the coming day. We will be calling on God often because so much can happen on these trips. We do not know how the students will truly respond when confronted in difficulty.

It is the second day of our trip. As expected all of the students were up and ready to go. The routine was becoming second nature so they all knew what they had to do.

The direction was to ascend the mountain which was gradual but elevated enough to challenge staying on your horse. Loose rocks would fall reminding us of the foundation that might be a bit unsure. The horses are usually very steady on their feet but loose gravel can take a horse off guard and possibly cause a fall, rider and all.

Not knowing where Robert and Ahoe were exactly going, they had a plan. As we climbed higher we could hear what sounded like a cat. In fact it sounded like more than one. As we looked up higher we could see two smaller cats playing among the rocks.

Being aware of their presence was extremely anxious because we knew the mother was close by. If the mother thought for a moment her babies were in trouble she would not hesitate for any reason. These mountain lion cats are adorable but make no mistake, mother will attack to kill.

We were warned to keep silent and to avoid the cats. As we climbed closer we tried to move farther away. They wanted to see us and what we were going to do. In the distance we could hear mother growling because she saw her babies gone out of the den. We could be in big trouble.

The best thing we could do was just ignore the babies and act as if they were not even there. Hopefully mother would see we were not threatening them. The babies continued to play and follow us. We kept moving watching in every direction.

The horses began to act up as though they were threatened. In our opinion of the mountain the footing was a bit unsure for the horses. They were moving awkwardly as if they knew trouble was near. We could hear the mother getting closer.

The best we could do at that moment was to pick up the pace and try to get away as far and as fast as we could. Robert and Ahoe led the way and Princess and I led behind. We could see if any of the students were in danger.

On an overhanging rock mother cat was standing and glaring as we passed under her position. At any moment she could jump and take anyone of us off our horse, injuring us as we fell. Mother could see that her babies were following and not being threatened. In the meantime, we moved as fast as we could but not trying to upset mother cat. She began to climb down and as she approached us she would hold her stance. I was the last one to go past her and she stayed secure on the rocks just above us.

The babies saw their mother and began to climb up to her. They were hungry and glad to see her. I believe the fact that the babies were left alone and we continued on our way ignoring them, mother knew they were safe. Any sudden moves and it could have been entirely different.

It was such a relief to have mother and babies out of sight. We were prepared to handle the situation as best as we could but we were very thankful we did not have too. We continued to ascend the mountain on our horses planning on reaching the top so we could camp for the night.

The scenery is awesome and as the sun came out the warmth felt wonderful on our faces. It was getting colder as we got closer to the top of the mountain. There were noises from birds, little creatures scurrying back and forth and a harmless snake basking on the rocks in the sun. Squirrels were quite prevalent and so were the chipmunks. We saw raccoons and skunks with an opossum or two.

The wind was picking up so we pulled out the jackets. It was time to prepare for dinner and making camp. It would be just a short time and we would reach the top. As we approached our campsite the view is unbelievable. You can see for miles into infinity. The ranch was out of our view because it was on the other side of the mountain.

We dismounted our horses, secured them, took the saddles off, gave them feed and water before we could have our own. We pitched our tents, gathered wood for the fire and looked for water. The designated cook for this meal started to prepare the food while the others did their own chores. Everyone had something to do.

After dinner and clean up we gathered around the campfire and we began to share. Robert who is usually quiet had some stories to tell. Ahoe contributed some of his and the students did share. These are the times that often a student will open up to get some resolution to a situation they have been carrying. We are all there to support and not criticize. They need to be accepted for who they are especially in this situation where our lives may depend on each other.

We also planned for the next day's trip. We were going to look for the waterfall and canoes where we can swim, canoe and fish if we choose to do so. Once it was dark we all headed for our tents to go to sleep. Robert and Ahoe would take turns keeping the fire burning to keep animals away and it would be ready for breakfast in the morning.

The trip that day was exhilarating, exhausting and tense with the mountain lions. Sleep was so easy to come by from each student. There was barely a sound from each tent as night began turning into morning. We could hear Robert and Ahoe getting each one up. Princess and I began getting breakfast while the others got dressed for the trip this day.

Breakfast is done, clean up is over, tents are packed and so is the camp. We extinguished the fire and then saddle the horses. We are getting good at this. By the end of the trip we will have it down to a science.

We need to descend half way down the mountain to find the water. As our horses are following our commands all is moving along smoothly. We are in single file when all of the sudden one of the students horse takes a tumble with the rider flying off his horse. In astonishment I moved forward to see what I could do. I got off my horse, ran to the student to see if there were any injuries. The horse managed to get up uninjured. The student lay unconscious briefly and then began to come around. Dazed by hitting his head on the fall he had blood running from his wound.

Calling for the first aid kit my priority is to deal with the apparent wound on his head. I stopped the bleeding, put on some medicine and then a bandage. He had a few more cuts and bruises but from what we could tell he was going to be alright.

We are all relieved that both horse and rider are okay. It took the other students by surprise but it was a good lesson in realizing that anytime something can happen you have no control over. We are ready to continue on our trip seeking out the water.

We must have been on horseback about two hours when we could hear the roaring sound of falling water, tons and tons of water. As we got closer we could feel the mist in the air as the water came crushing down to the rocks below. The back wash of the water as it flew back into the air was carried away in the wind. This is the pleasurable feeling of mist that saturated the air. It was wonderful.

We came to the clearing and the sun was shinning. A rainbow crossed the water to the other side. The trees surrounding the falls were so moist and green. They have a continual drink of water. Flowers are in bloom in their wild nature and so beautiful. Birds are flying over head as if to welcome us. You feel as though you would want to stay here forever.

There is a clearing that is perfect for camp. We can set up wind so we do not get wet with the moist water coming from the falls. It may be difficult to find dry firewood but I am sure we will manage.

First it is lunchtime and then we can play. It has to be swimming and jumping off the rocks into deep enough water. We can all swim so it should be fun. Our wounded student has to take it easy but there is nothing that says he cannot swim if he takes it easy.

The horses even decided to take a swim. After we removed the riding gear they were free to do as they pleased. A drink was great and so was the swim. There was plenty of grass for them to graze on. You treat your horse like a first class citizen. He is your companion on a trip like this. You depend on him for everything especially finding home if you get lost. Most horses can find their way home at great distances.

We decided to get closer to the falls and see if we could get a shower where the water was not falling to severely. We struggled on the rocks to make our way closer to the falls. Once we got there we tried to go under the falls. Would you believe it but there was a cave under the falls. There was some water falling and then as you got through that you could enter the cave.

This was exciting and we were anxious to explore. We called Robert, Ahoe then Princess and I got the other students. This was an investigating experience with such a sense of curiosity. What would we find and how far can we go? We did equip ourselves with flashlights so we would follow Robert and Ahoe. I was happy to let them go first.

We could hear some noise inside the cave. The smell was that of cold wet dirt. The dampness was particularly chilling. There was some water dripping down the walls. We started to sense a smell of animal but we were not sure. We could hear the sound get a little louder.

As we went deeper into the cave Robert could shine his light ahead to see if he could determine what it was. As we walked closer he could see thousands of bats hanging in the cave. They are just waiting for nightfall so they can come out. Robert told us not to be afraid because these bats would not hurt us. In fact they will eat the insects at night so we would not be bothered by them. We were stepping on the bat dung which I guess that was to be expected.

As we retrieved from the cave we passed through the water again to the other side. There is one area that the water is not flowing over the side where the bats can come out of the cave. This was all so fascinating and interesting. We will be serenaded by the bats that evening as we bed down for the night.

We continued to swim, splash and jump into the water. It was getting close to dinner time so we had to do our chores, eat dinner and go to sleep that night. As was predicted the bats did come out, soaring in the air for food, and it was a serenade to behold. Believe it or not we went to sleep with this wonderful sound.

The next morning after breakfast the plan was to canoe down the river and then we would walk back with the canoes over our heads. The continual thought would be that as far down as you paddle the same distance you have to walk back. The canoes are stored here for more students on camping trips. There would be two to a canoe and a paddle for each student.

Some decided to fish so their journey would not be as far. They could tie up or fish on the side of the river. There were many options and choices to be made. Again Princess and I would follow in the last position so we could see what was happening up ahead. Our responsibility was to help any of the students in any situation that needed assistance. We were prepared for most any thing that might go array.

As were got our assigned canoes, the pairings were set and the decisions were made as to what canoe would be chosen for the student to take. Robert and Ahoe split up in the canoes so that we could see them at all times.

The full journey was about 20 miles down stream. We did pack overnight gear in case the trip back on foot was too far for the rest of the day. Lunch and dinner were packed in case fish were not caught. A fisherman knows never to completely depend on his or hers skill to fill the hungry tummy. The thought of fresh fish over the open fire was pretty exciting.

The canoes started their decent into the water. They have been trained how to maintain their balance while both getting into the canoe. One of the students would step in and secure themselves and the other would steady the canoe. The second student steps in while the first one holds steady. He secures the canoe with his paddle firmly anchored into the ground by holding it firm against the ground.

All is going well when the current began a bit more convincing and a canoe began turning down stream. This in itself is not a problem but the students were not safe. As the canoe began turning the students lost their balance and over they both went into the water. The canoe began down stream overturned and floating at quite a good speed.

They managed to hold on and ride out the overturned canoe by holding on to the sides. They were both on the same side to encourage each other. They did not panic and they saw the contents of their canoe floating downstream. This is not the priority at the moment but will be later if they cannot retrieve everything.

What we wanted to do was assist in catching up to them. The water was running pretty good so we had to pick up speed. Princess and I work well together and have a lot of experience. If they would stay calm and try not to fight the moving water they will be better off.

We accelerated our speed by moving the paddles at a faster pace. The ability to anticipate your partner's moves is critical in doing what had to be done. We were gaining momentum and the overturned canoe was getting closer. We managed to pull along side the canoe and hold to it by the rope we had in the canoe. We could secure the two canoes so the students could get their bearings and make their way over to us for help.

The depth of the water varied significantly as you would expect in a river. Hopefully there may be sandbars ahead which could be just the answer. The canoes ahead knew we were in trouble with the overturned canoes. They were able to rescue the supplies floating down the river. Everything was meant to float.

The lead canoe with Robert and Ahoe did get the word about what was happening. They found an adequate sandbar that we could hold ourselves and bring the canoe upright. The river is such that there was not an appropriate spot to tie up the canoes. The shoreline was either too high or too dangerous. This is wilderness.

Each canoe made a place to secure, get out and hold the canoe still. We were coming down with the overturned canoe and ours attached to it. The sandbar went across the river so there was a large enough area for all of us to function and do what we needed to do.

The plan worked, the students were fine but wet and their lost supplies were returned to them. It was fortunate that the food basket handles were crossed in such a manner that the lid stayed closed while floating down the river. The paddles were held on to by the students. In fact, they helped to secure them while holding onto the boat.

It all happened so fast but fortunately we were prepared and it did turn out okay. A few cuts and bruises from what was in the river were expected. They were not able to get a footing with the fast running currant. We got all the canoes ready to continue on our trip.

The view is awesome. We can see deer with their young, small animals that live by the water, and in clear water you can see the trout swimming. This is such a beautiful way to experience nature at its best.

We all decided to try to fish. We needed a clearing where we could bank the canoe, prepare our fishing equipment and fish from shore. Robert and Ahoe know of the perfect spot. We even have a campfire so we can cook the fish we catch.

The area is found, we paddle to secure the canoes and get out. This is probably the only sandy area on the entire river bank. Actually Robert and Ahoe had made this area for the students on these camping trips. The purpose was so they can learn to catch fish, clean them and then eat them. We were going to camp out for the night and continue in the morning.

All of the students did know how to fish, bait their hook and clean the fish. Each one would take turn with each chore. Robert and Ahoe are in charge of the process as the students followed their lead.

We dug for worms, prepared our poles (nothing fancy just string, a hook and a pole) which were made out of broken branches. You toss your line out into the water; the currant will carry it downstream and wait for the catch. The water is plentiful of fish so this should not take too long.

We started fishing, the fire is being prepared and the fry pan is getting warm. This is not going to take too long. The knives are being sharpened and ready for cleaning.

It did not take long when the first strike was hit by a fish. The tug and pull was exciting and the best part was getting it to shore. This was done and fish #1 is the first to be put into the pan after preparation. We went searching for berries to add to our dinner. We do have emergency rations but we would rather do this meal with what we find.

Some of the rations were potatoes which we threw into the fire. They taste so good after you break through the burnt crusted covering and get to the meat of the potato. It is amazing how your appetite changes to accommodate the situation you are in. You will eat things that you probably would not ordinarily or it just tastes so much better.

We had plenty of food, clean up was over, a little time by the fire and then it was time for bed. We were going to sleep out in the open with just our bed role. The night was beautiful, the stars glistened like diamonds and the sound of the evening atmosphere was melodic. Between the bats looking for food or the noises of the insects, it put us all asleep.

After breakfast, packing the canoes and clearing out our campsite for the next occupants, we were back in the water. We were confident that there would not be another turned over canoe. The first experience was enough to make everyone aware of how easily things can happen.

The first hour has passed and our journey is even better than the day before. The weather is beautiful; the scenery is as if a painter had painted the landscape just to accommodate us. It is amazing.

As we continue down stream our destination is to meet at the end of the river and walk back to the waterfalls where we had left. We were going to basically snack as hunger began to trigger our stomachs. We had plenty to choose from and no one would get hungry until we found camp for the night. Robert and Ahoe knew what we were looking for and how far it was. We trusted them with our lives literally.

As the time passed and we were enjoying the trip and each other we could feel the temperature in the air become colder. The wind started to pick up and it was moving against us. We started paddling harder and it became more difficult. As we looked up into the sky the clouds began to form and become darker. The thought that came into my mind is that a storm is brewing.

The air became damp and colder. The wind continued to push against us. We paddled harder and our canoe began to turn. We tried to stop the turning but the force of the wind was gaining momentum. As we were pushed sideways we were moving into the canoe ahead. In fact all the canoes were in trouble. They look like dodgem cars at the carnival.

The rain started forcibly pushing directly at us. It hurt as it made contact with our face. We managed to put on a waterproof jacket we packed but the rest of our body was exposed. It was hard to hold onto the canoe but the best thing we could do was ride out the storm. Our prayer was that we would not be struck by lightening.

Thunder began to roar throughout the sky and then we could see lightening. It was pretty close to us and being in the water was anything but ideal. Our priority was to get out of the water and find shelter. We have to protect the canoes as best we can because they are our transportation to camp.

The thunder continued, the wind kept blowing us and the water was very angry with what was happening. It wanted to settle down but the elements would not let it. There was a terrific flash of lightening and we could hear a tree split from a bolt of lightening. Up ahead the split tree crashed to the ground falling over the river at this point. We could not tell if this was a good thing or not until we reach the place the fallen tree was put to rest.

Our canoes are still out of control as we are hanging on; we could not paddle to set us in any kind of a direction. All we could do is ride the water as it took us along. We were fast approaching the fallen tree when Robert and Ahoe would reach the place first. They would give us direction and help as to what we should do next.

The tree is large enough to climb up on and pull our canoes over to the river edge. The hard rain made it difficult to maneuver but necessary for us to get off the river. We had little choice. Robert set the pattern for us to follow and with each other helping we accomplished the task. We all were able to cross the fallen tree, secure our canoes, and wait out the storm as soon as we found shelter.

There was an opening in the rocks that made a great shelter from the lightening. We were stranded from continuing our trip for a couple of hours. In the meantime, we could make a fire with dry wood hidden from the rain. We brought our supplies with us as we got out of the canoes. It was such a relief to be hidden from the outside where it was so dangerous. Also we had each other to share this experience.

The weather cleared, we packed up what we had used and put it in the canoes. We were back on the water and it had changed its character. It was back welcoming us our trip down the river. It was in a much better mood now that the threats of thunder, rain and lightening have passed.

The rest of the trip was delightful. We reached camp where we were to spend the night. We made the fire, cooked dinner, exhausted from our trip and fast asleep. It was as if all that had happen seemed to be a dream and we were a part of it. The difference is that is was all real and there are witnesses to the fact. We have all matured since the beginning of this trip which is the purpose of this camping trip.

It is daybreak; we all get up, pack, eat and break camp. We are going to carry our canoes back to the waterfalls about 20 miles. It will take a day or two depending upon a lot of things. If everything is ideal it will be just that. If there are problems, it will take longer. We are looking forward to the trip back on foot but we do not know how the weight of the canoe over our heads will be. We will just take one thing at a time.

We have managed 5 miles and we set up camp for lunch. We did take a few breaks just to relax our muscles. This break is a much needed welcomed time. We are going to take a little longer than usual because the strain has been more trying.

The campsite is prepared for our stop and time to refresh. We are by the water and some decided to swim. The storm from the day before has turned this day into a beautiful summer day. The temperature outside is perfect and the temperature in the water is awesome. We are going to take full advantage of this moment.

It is time to move on and put some more miles behind us. We are refreshed and eager to continue so we can reach the waterfall by evening. This may or may not be possible but we are trying to get there by nightfall.

The trail is pretty obvious as though many people have gone through here many times. You could see remnants of their presence by messages or rock formation left for those like us to see that they were here. Somehow we feel that moment has importance. Perhaps it is sharing an intimate moment with a stranger. We all have a story to tell.

We stopped for dinner and then to our amazement we did make it to the waterfall by night time. We were so relieved to put down the canoes for good. At that moment we wished we would never see a canoe again. I know this will change but right now this is how we felt. We have had too much to do with the canoe. It literally became a part of us.

The horses were glad to see us and so were we. We did take time to spend with them and then we had to unpack so we could set up camp again. We were going to spend another day here just swimming and relaxing and riding our horses if we want. A wonderful day off will be a great reward from the great canoe journey.

We did take the next day to refresh, relax and prepare to go home. We have been challenged in so many ways but the best part was seeing how we all worked together, thought alike and experienced things for a lifetime remembrance.

The trip home was routine as we made the large circle back to the ranch. We went down the mountain and arrived at the ranch in a couple days. It did seem faster coming home but that is just the illusion of having a great time. We are anxious to get back to regular meals, clean up and prepare for the students to go home. This experience is the best way to teach anyone the limitations of their character and what they are made of.

All my friends greeted Lucky Jo and I. There is nothing like home in any place but especially when it is your home. We took care of the horses first, unloaded our gear and cleaned everything ready for the next time. We always do the work first so that we do not have it hanging over our heads and it is done.

CHAPTER 10: Some More Fun

The Parade

Once a year on Labor Day there is a parade in the nearest town about eleven miles away and we are asked to participate. We enjoy this because we have a chance to show off the many facets of the ranch. It gives us an opportunity to let those visiting for the summer to know what we have available that they can take advantage of for them or their family member.

Chief and his family are also an exciting participation of the parade. They display their Indian heritage by displaying their tradition costumes. It also brings awareness to the Indian reservation which they live next to at the edge of our property. They are such an important part of the uniqueness and atmosphere which makes this area so special.

The other ranchers contribute to make this an expected event which is looked forward to every year. Each ranch has something different to offer in there own way. In this part of the country it is a perfect example of what life was like many years ago. Fortunately for us we have the modern conveniences available which helps us do a better job.

I am riding Lucky Jo and he loves the music. It has to be in his blood because he holds his head up high, prances as though he were "The Stud" of all times, and gives me the ride of a Queen if that were my status in life. This is so much fun because he has a chance to show off the awesome character of his stature. He is still and always will be the most special horse in the whole world, bar none.

The streets are lined with people. You can see the cheers and tears of the children as we pass by. We have apples to pass out from our orchards and they look forward to this. This is one of the best parts of the parade. The children try to cross the roped area but they do respect the boundaries.

After the parade we gather in an area so that the families can have personal contact with us and the horses. Our horses are used to people because of the work they do on the ranch. This also gives the families an up close and personal experience with us and the ranch. Uncle Nick is a great representative of the ranch and people are drawn to him. Robert also is quiet but a wonderful person on the ranch. His knowledge is so obvious as soon as he speaks.

After all the festivities, we embark on the journey home. This is a fun ride home. We take the highway for part of the journey and then we are able to cross over onto our land. We all have a great time.

Chief and his family disembark part way to go to their home. The other ranchers start to pair off going to their homes. We continue on until we reach our ranch. This was an awesome day and probably better than last year. Of course we say that every year and think that it is true.

The Apple Orchard

Another yearly event in the fall is picking apples in the orchard. We open it up to the public so we can share our crop and abundance. We pick apples to sell and to use. It is more fun to fill up the wagons and take others out so they can pick their own.

The children particularly love this experience. They have more fun running through the trees, jumping over the fallen apples and finding the perfect one to eat.

They gather apples by the bushel so they can take them home for their own personal use. Moms love the apples for baking, canning and just plain eating. They have to be stored in their fruit cellar in the ground to last a long time.

One particular family we look forward to every year. They have twelve children, six of their own and six adopted with special needs. They are remarkable as a family and work together as a unit. They look out for each other giving assistance whenever needed.

They have a wagon and fill it up just by the numbers. Some of the children are not able to pick the apples but that does not matter. They still have a job for each one. They all can pick an apple from the ground and put it in the bushel basket. Some of them are slower than others but still can contribute. This size family needs a lot of apples and we can accommodate them. We love the opportunity.

We make our way back to the ranch and help unload the wagon. Most of the children do the work. The others help one another. They are such a blessing to help and to witness as you see this special family loving one another. They truly are special and so the parents have reached out beyond themselves and God has given them the provision mentally, physically and emotionally to cope. This is a reward in itself just to witness God's provision for them.

The Pumpkin Patch

We also plant pumpkins for the fall planting which we use for our own needs plus the needs of others. We open up the pumpkin patch to those ranches around us for the

Halloween festivities. The children love getting on the wagons and looking for their perfect pumpkin to pick.

As the wagon goes out the excitement begins to escalate. The families are having more fun searching and playing on the wagon. We have limited rules such as no pushing off the wagon and not too much straw thrown. Besides that it is pretty much just having fun.

After a few passes in the wagon the perfect pumpkin is spotted. They jump off the wagon and reach the one. We accommodate with the clippers to cut the pumpkin from the vine. Everyone is happy and back to the ranch we go.

This is the ritual all day long. Now that the air is getting colder greeting fall, the horses enjoy the change in temperature. They become a bit frisker and start to grow their winter coat. This protection is necessary and it changes the look of the horse. When spring comes and the coat begins to shed and they return to the look we are most familiar with.

The Christmas Tree Cutting

There are some evergreens on the property that are perfect Christmas trees. Having them cut down is good so that the others have room to grow. We open up the ranch at Christmas time for those who would like to cut down their own Christmas tree.

We load up the wagon again and take the families out to find the perfect Christmas tree. Dad and mom see a tree differently than the children. Children do not care if it is long or tall, short or fat, a lot of branches or a few, their idea is from the heart. This is where mom and dad have to supervise especially getting it into the house to decorate.

After the approval of mom and dad, we execute the cutting down ceremony so we can tie up the tree to the wagon and drag it back to the ranch. Everyone gets a chance to take a few cuts at the trunk of the tree and the proper direction to do the cutting. When we hear timber we know the job is done.

We tie up the tree and back to the ranch for the next family. This is also great fun and my Aunt has hot chocolate and cookies waiting by a fire. These memories will last for a lifetime and probably continued with the children and their families.

The Wagon Rides

We have wagon rides which in themselves are so much fun. They are purposed to go a distance, have a campfire, cook over the fire and return back to the ranch. This is a couple hour journey and loved by all.

We have a place that is perfect for this set up. It is by the river bank and the area is safe for the fire. The area has been cleared away so that by the river bank you can fish or even swim if it is warm enough. There are enough creatures there to keep you busy for more than a day.

As we reached our destination and unloaded the wagon we came upon a raccoon and her family. We know that raccoons can be dangerous but we also know enough not to disturb or threaten the family.

As we came closer mother and babies did retreat into the woods. Fortunately for us they just came down for a drink. Had they set up house keeping it could have been much worse. It could have been a territorial war. This is very dangerous and we would have had to leave.

The weather was too cold to swim but we had a great time by the water, cooking over the fire, and just hanging out. It was time to go back to the ranch but it was a great time for all on the wagon.

CHAPTER 11: My Aunt and Uncle Would Be Proud

Reflecting back on the years that have gone by and the years ahead, my Aunt Millie and Uncle Nick would be proud of their decision to Will me the ranch. The years spent on the ranch in my childhood prepared me for making the transition of becoming owner and operator. The legacy of The Me'chus Dynasty is a privilege I honor and am so thankful for this opportunity.

I could not have imagined that this fantasy of mine would be a reality in many years to come. It is rare that so many dreams are never realized. Without dreams to believe in life there would be little hope for your future.

The effect we have had on all our neighbors is such a joy and a blessing. The fact that we have been effective in so many people's lives is what this ranch was meant to be by my Aunt and Uncle. The fact that my Uncle was an immigrant, he spent his life loving this country and helping others. His legacy may not be known to all those in the world but it is certainly embraced by those he has helped.

In the early days our neighbors were more dependent on each other. As the ranch grew and developed we became more self sufficient but we still communicated with our neighbors and we were always there for each other.

After taking over the ranch and being so familiar with the people and operation surrounding us, I could continue what they had started. This is what they wanted and this is why they left the ranch to me.

Lucky Jo

Looking back at this precious friend not able to begin to tell of the feelings for this wonderful horse, he has been my life. The realization that there will be a time that his life may come to an end, but until that time I will love him and care for him as much as if he were my child that I have raised.

He has been a devoted companion, brother, friend, intimate soul mate and anything else you could describe as someone who is your life. The fact that I have never married is the indication that Lucky Jo supplied me with a relationship as close to being my husband as possible. All my pets and relationships are my family. Trusting them with my life and they can trust me also.

Lucky Jo is a bit slower, his eye sight not as keen, and not as frisky as he used to be. He can take a journey but not as far anymore. Respecting his age and his needs at this point, is no different than for others.

Kelly and Fudzer

Kelly has been the dog everyone dreams about. She is obedient, intelligent and faithful. Her days on the ranch have been well spent in doing her duties and just being a loving companion. The relationship between Lucky Jo and Fudzer is that they are family to each other.

Kelly does not do the rounding up of the horses like she used to but she still commands attention from the new horses in the corral. As long as she can she will be who she is and contribute when she can. She stays close to Lucky Jo and Fudzer as they hang out together. They wonder about but stay pretty close to home.

I take them to Chief, Tamar, Ahoe and Princess as much as possible. We are all family and it is like visiting your relatives when we make the trip. Ahoe and Princess have their own families now and they teach on the Reservation. They both have children and we love spending time with them. They all live close to their parents so in this close proximity we can see them often.

Fudzer does not jump as high as she used to or catch the mice we appreciated when she eliminated them for us. She is showing the years also but just as important as ever. To see her around reminds us of the days of old when we all ran and played from dawn to dusk. I cannot do that anymore myself.

Robert

Robert is getting up in years. He does not always make his appearance as early as he used to. He keeps more to himself now and I think his health is failing. Asking him about something which is out of character for his actions and he just passes it off as "Just getting older". Not prying too deeply as to what this means, but realize that time is not on his side anymore.

With Robert's limitations are fine because as long as he is with me, there is a sense of things still the same. If God should decide that it is his time to die I do not want to even think of that but will accept it. He has been my mother, father, sister, brother, aunt and uncle since they passed away. All that has been accomplished since inheriting the ranch could not have been accomplished if it was not for him.

Me

While telling my story, my writing has been when an opportunity would arise. Many of the stories are related to the ranch, many of the people who are and have been a part of it and I have been writing for the local newspaper.

My many interesting subjects to draw a perfect story line, has been received by local human interest, over the United States or even world wide. The technical abilities of technology at my disposal have made it possible for me to travel without leaving the ranch.

As a freelance writer there are no responsibilities to any boss or company. My contributions can be submitted to a wide variety of places. My allegiance is to bring about interest, answer questions the reader may have and do research which is accessible through the internet.

In my early years as a writer, discovering travel was one of the best ways to find my way through a developing journey. Such a varied collection of people at my disposal and each one has a story to tell. This is probably the one thing in common with most people is that they have a story to tell. They just need someone who is will to listen and show value in what they have to say.

Each person's life has meaning too many people but so often they do not realize that and feel abandoned by their families. Often too much has been said or too much time has interfered with the ability to come back together and mend fences that are broken.

I will continue to write as long as my mind and my hands hold out. It seems that my thoughts create interesting patterns that can be another story to tell. There is a never ending series of things that happen and you could spend an eternity writing about them. Who would be around to read it or even care by then? Actually I plan to be in heaven with Jesus.

The Perfect Place

The Me'chus Dynasty is the perfect place in this world and so thankful to have been a part of its growing up and sustaining itself. Much of me is in the ranch so when the time comes that we have to put it in the hands of another, our heritage will certainly be remembered by the places we have put our stamp of acknowledgement.

The wild horses are still a part of the structure in the vast amount of acres we call ours. Still not knowing the number of acers, it is large. Most of the ranches in this area are a combination of many acres, trees, water and trails to find your way across the lands. There are really no restrictions unless you mean harm. We are all familiar with our neighbors even though their ranch may be many miles away.

The wild dogs still roam the lands but do not appear too often. They pretty much stay to themselves knowing that it is the safest for the pack. Food is abundant in the hills and valleys so they do not wander close to the ranch to find food such as our chickens and small animals for food. The pigs and piglets so far have been safe and our calves have been raised to adult to provide food for us for the season. The balance of nature on the ranch is a God given ability for the ranch to support us.

The horses are bred and bought as a business. They are also used for riding purposes. Occasionally we have an exceptional horse born that is worth a lot of money. He or she is kept away from the other horses until it can be protected from danger. All our horses are valuable but some need a little more attention than others. When auction time comes the competition is very tense and we want to produce a great specimen for show and to be bid on.

We still have the visiting children, those that want to learn to ride and those who want to learn to ride their own horse. This is a great opportunity for them to become very efficient on horseback. It can mean life or death out here if you do not know how to ride or survive is some pretty obscure areas. The deer roam without fear of being shot because we do not allow hunting on the property. Some ranchers do allow hunting to keep some of the deer from starving in the winter. This weeding out or thinning out the herd is necessary so more can survive. The meat is necessary for the winter storage of food.

To preserve the food for winter we cut chunks of ice that have formed near the center of the river. The river will continue to flow all year round but the edges will form ice. We take this ice, dig a deep area in the ground, and surround it with the chunks of ice to make an ice house. The cold dirt insulates the ice so it stays frozen to store the food so it does not spoil.

I consider this the perfect place. It has so much to offer and so much to give. To be a part of this and then to inherit it is a child's dream come true. If I were able to design my life from my pen and paper it would have been just like this. Of course the mysteries have to be told because if you knew what was going to happen what fun would there be in writing about it.

www.ingramcontent.com/pod-product-compliance
Lightning Source LLC
LaVergne TN
LVHW011353080426
835511LV00005B/270